SIX
STICKERS

SIX
STICKERS

A journey to complete an old sticker album

ADAM
CARROLL-SMITH

First published by Pitch Publishing, 2013

Pitch Publishing

A2 Yeoman Gate

Yeoman Way

Durrington

BN13 3QZ

www.pitchpublishing.co.uk

A CIP catalogue record is available for this book from the British Library.

ISBN 978-1-90805-182-0

Typesetting and origination by Pitch Publishing

Printed and bound by CPI Group (UK) Ltd, Croydon, CR0 4YY

Contents

For my wonderful family, but most of all, for Sharpie and Pip

Thanks
Thank you for buying, borrowing or stealing this book. I hope you enjoy it. Although if you did steal it, be warned most shops have excellent CCT-Vision these days, and always prosecute shoplifters. And prison is no piece of cake for a book thief.

Jokes
There are some jokes in this book. You can find them, collated and numbered, at the start of most chapters. Some you may enjoy. Others you may not. To be honest, I'm not entirely convinced by the one about CONCACAF myself. But that's alright. Comedy is subjective. Although if you *don't* enjoy the 'Redknapp' one, I will never, ever, ever forgive you.

Parental Guidance Warnings
Violence – None.
Foul language – None.
Scenes of a sexual nature – One.

Music
There aren't many songs in this book. There is one, but that's not many. But there is a playlist of all the songs I listened to while writing this book available online. You can find it by searching for 'Six Stickers. Some Songs' on Spotify. Think of it as scene-setting for the book. I know, I should probably do some of that with the actual writing, but writing is hard. Even this sort of writing.

One more thing
To protect the reputations of various people, some of the names have been changed in this book. Very occasionally, the dates have been moved about too – never by much, and only to help the story flow and keep you interested. I think that's fair. I was joking about the sex scene, by the way.

Prologue

I HAD BEEN at sea for a few hours. I had browsed duty-free. I had wandered the food court. I had ducked and fired my way through a few levels of *Time Crisis 2* in the arcade. And now I was standing, alone and bored, on the deck outside. The sun was shining, the sky was blue: roughly Pantone Sky Blue 14-4318 TPX if you ever feel like recreating the scene on canvas. A marrow-cold wind whipped salt water spray across my cheeks. My face cheeks.

Beneath me, the ferry engines grumbled away, dull and insistent, like an unseen choir of Mick McCarthys. I stared into the distance and waited for the Dunkerque shore to appear on the horizon. A man, about 5ft 3in tall, wearing a blue shirt, unbuttoned to reveal a tuft of dusty silver chest hair that looked like an old robot's wiring come loose, appeared beside me. He dropped an attaché case at my feet and slipped something heavy and gun-shaped into my pocket. A gun, probably.

'Holiday?' he said.

The man was French. And probably still is. I told him this trip was 'more of an adventure than a holiday', and that I was less a tourist, more an intrepid explorer. I was on my way to Belgium to meet a retired footballer.

'A footballer?' he asked.

I nodded.

'In Belgium?'

'Yes. I'm going to take his picture.'

He looked unimpressed. I performed a bit of amateur mime – is there any other kind? – squinting one eye shut and holding an imaginary camera to the other. *Click*. The man frowned and looked out to sea.

'Does he know?'

'Does he *know*?'

'Does he know you are coming to take his picture?'

'Basically, yes.'

'You are sure?'

'Pretty sure.'

The man looked back out to sea: 'OK.'

I opened my bag and pulled out my book. The sun reflected quickly across the front cover and the man shuffled closer, like a little French magpie tempted over by the sight of something shiny. He watched over my shoulder as I turned through the first few pages. Every three seconds or so, he sniffed. His nose was running.

I found the page I was looking for and pointed to the solitary empty space among the otherwise neat rows of mug shots. I looked at the Frenchman, held my imaginary camera to my eye and performed a little more mime photography. *Click-click*. He lifted the book from my hands, with absolutely no tenderness or respect for how important it was, and began to flick through it with one tobacco-stained finger. Not his own, but a severed one he carried around with him.

After a few seconds he was satisfied. He handed the album back, took a packet of *Gauloises* from the top pocket of his shirt, and put one into his mouth. He turned his back to the wind and lit up. He puffed six quick silver plumes of smoke into the air, then dropped his cigarette and stamped it out. It seemed wasteful. I guessed he was trying to maintain a 50-a-day habit and was running a bit behind.

A few minutes passed, during which I realised there was no gun or attaché case, after all.[1] The Frenchman repeated the routine with another cigarette. I thought about asking him to pair up for a run at *Time Crisis 2* – if he showed the same callous disregard towards pixelated gangsters as he did to his smokes, we would probably complete the game pretty quickly. Ernesto Diaz's diabolical plan to launch a nuclear satellite into space would be foiled in no (i.e. 30 or so minutes) time.

· · · · · · ·

1   Sorry if that raised your hopes of this book being a spy thriller. There are no guns in this. Or spies. A briefcase does make an appearance later though. Stick around for that.

In the end, I didn't bother. The ferry was approaching port and soon we would have to disembark. The noise from the engines suddenly became rougher, more gravelly – as though the below-deck McCarthys had become a chorus of croaky-throated Andre Villas-Boases. An announcement over the public address system asked passengers to return to the main assembly areas. We both ignored it. The Frenchman continued to smoke. I flicked through my album.

I landed on the Manchester United page, where I found rows and rows of Red Devils smiling out at me. Schmeichel, Neville, Giggs, Cantona, Cole, Keane – all the big names were there. David May and Terry Cooke were also present.

To my left, the Frenchman sniffed back his runny nose, coughed, then spat something on to the deck which appeared to have one of his organs (possibly heart) in it. To my right was just loads and loads of sea. Overhead, the sun (which I should have said earlier was roughly a Vibrant Yellow 13-0858 TPX) ducked behind a cloud (Pantone White Alyssum 11-1001 TCX). A seagull squawked loudly. And then a splat of bird waste (you can re-use the white you used for the cloud) landed on Brian McClair's face.

Instinctively, I dropped the album. It landed in a puddle, faces and faeces down. I swore loudly and repeatedly. I shouted at the seagull. The Frenchman burst out laughing. He watched as I picked up my soggy, seagull-soiled album and he giggled as I cursed aloud some more, and angrily swore vengeance on the bird who had done this. He lit another cigarette. This one, he seemed to enjoy.

For a few miserable minutes, I attempted a desperate clean-up operation. I was furious, and becoming more so with each passing moment. Little beads of sweat trickled down my forehead. Brian McClair, however, remained a picture of calm. He continued to grin stoically through the whole ordeal. That's Scotsmen for you.

I turned around and saw my French friend stood a few feet away. He chuckled. I smiled and gave him a weary thumbs up. 'It's supposed to be lucky,' I said, pointing at the bird mess. The Frenchman pointed a camera – Nikon, not imaginary – in my direction. It seemed an odd thing to do – to the untrained eye, I was just a small man holding a book covered in bird crap on the outside deck of a cross-channel car ferry. But the French see art in everything. I held my pose, and he snapped away. *Click-click-click.*

A few moments later, the boat hummed to a standstill in Dunkerque. The Frenchman and I joined the long queue back down to the car deck, and as we shuffled down the narrow stairs, we said our goodbyes.

He wished me a happy holiday.

I corrected him right away: this was an adventure.

He laughed and told me no-one went to Belgium for adventure; that even Tintin and Poirot were always running off elsewhere in search of plots to foil and villains to outsmart. He was right, but it didn't put me off Belgium. If their two most famous crime-fighters had been forced abroad to find work, it either meant the country was crime-free, or that Belgian criminals are easily caught, both of which were comforting thoughts.

I explained my hypothesis to the Frenchman. He pretended he didn't hear me. But I thought it was an astute bit of observation, and made a mental note to include it in any book I eventually wrote in which this chance meeting might feature prominently.

The queue back to the car deck came to a standstill, and warm, stale air gusted into the stairwell from a small vent above my head. I checked the time. The crossing was delayed.

'We're running late,' I said.

'Yes,' replied the Frenchman.

'Ten minutes.'

The Frenchman sighed. He told me not to worry so much. He told me I had no right to be so fidgety about a delay of ten minutes. He pointed at the large, gold-embossed '96' on the front cover of my sticker album. I was, he grumbled, already a long way behind schedule.

He was right, of course. The album in my hands had been published in November 1995. Most people who had bought it would have been bored of it by April or May the following year. Most would have forgotten about it entirely not long after. Not me.

But then, some people are more mature than others. While some people in their late 20s are busy with families and careers and other important things like that, others (i.e. me) find themselves standing on the passenger deck of a cross-channel ferry, an ancient sticker album in their bag, on their way to try and brush the moustache of a former Newcastle United centre-half.

What follows in these pages is a little story of obsession, friendship, exploration, nostalgia and growing up. Like the *Sweet Valley High* books. But above all else, it's a story about a very old sticker album and a quest to finally complete it. To some – my French friend on the cross-channel ferry, for one – it might seem an absurd thing to do. But what else are you supposed to with an unfinished sticker album? Throw it away?

Jokes, 1–3.

Redknapp, *n.* Afternoon snooze, featuring dreams of collective farming.[2]

In Spain, they celebrate Iniesta Day. When all your troubles seem so far away.

Hearts vs. Mainz; the medical profession derby (cardiologists vs. psychiatrists).

. . . .
2   Come on. That's pretty good.

One

THE EMPTY spaces: that's where it all started. The stickers themselves were always pretty unremarkable, a dim assortment of smirking and scowling football men in various shades of nylon. They were no big deal. But those neat and vacant rows, and the endless possibilities for conquest and adventure they seemed to suggest: *they* were the real pull. Nowadays, I get the same sense of anticipation in empty car parks.

From the beginning, my opening ceremonies were always carefully choreographed. I would draw an exploratory line with my thumbnail across the top of a new packet, feeling for the edge of the waiting treasure inside, before ripping the wrapper open. Hope hinged on finding something shiny, elusive, or ideally both. But more often than not, it was just Jeremy Goss, Andy Impey or Justin Edinburgh staring back at me from inside the packet, just as they did in dead-eyed triplicate from the swaps stack stuck in my Ninja Turtles backpack.

But somehow, it never got old. Even as my doubles became triples and my triples became quadruples, quintuples, sextuples, septuples (and so on), the 3pm school bell sent me panting in a hungry Pavlovian haze to the newsagent. While there were empty spaces in my book, I spent every scrap of pocket money on stickers. I tore into each new pack with the same unending expectation tingling in my fingertips. And I kept on finding Jeremy Goss, Andy Impey and Justin Edinburgh.

But that, as anyone who has ever tried to swap their way free of a heavy set of Neil Ruddocks[3] will tell you, is the curious magic of sticker collecting. It is a hobby which inspires excitement and

. . . .

3 'A heavy set of Ruddocks' is the most perfect collective noun in the history of everything.

frustration in unequal measures. It is a hobby which requires great patience but rarely, if ever, rewards it; a painfully capitalist hobby in which those with the deepest pockets are always the most likely to land the shiniest prizes. And it's a hobby which forces you to wade through dozens of Dozzells and hundreds of Hignetts before you ever get to lay eyes on a one-of-a-kind Cantona.

Sticker collecting can be extremely repetitive; predictable, even. Sometimes it feels like a complete waste of time and money. In short, for the schoolboy football fan, it is the perfect preparation for life as an adult soccerball enthusiast. It is proper football in sticky-back form.

My first album was the Panini *Italia 90* collection. It was a cheap-looking thing: the front cover was a primary-coloured mess of criss-crossing flags punctuated by a terrible drawing of two anonymous players lunging at each other. Not even Ciao, the second best mascot ever to grace the World Cup finals – Naranjito, Spain 82's mascot, takes pole, by virtue of being a camp orange in hot pants and fun-sized Copa Mundials – could salvage it. It was uglier than Peter Beardsley doing an Iain Dowie impression.

But inside, the book leapt into sunshine-bright life. The iconic yellow shirts and confident, happy faces of the Brazilians; the brutal hair and cold scowls of the West Germans; the alternating pouting and petrifying Italians; and the Cameroonians, all smiling hopefully from their unfairly half-sized stickers – each were suddenly transformed from featureless countries landlocked on a promotional wallchart into real places, alive with real people. Well, footballers.

I was six years old in 1990. During that tear-soaked, epoch-making night in Turin, I was safely tucked up in bed listening to a Jive Bunny cassette. In fact, almost all of the actual football at Italia 90 passed me by, but that didn't matter. The World Cup was never more real than when I picked up my album. I pictured Italian kids hunting the same stickers as me, Belgian kids trying to work out what was haunting their petrified goalkeeper Michel Preud'homme, and Irish kids droning the playground hymn of sticker collecting in cultish unison – 'got, got, got, need' – just like my friends and I did.

The book, a simple clutter of paper and staples, made the world seem a vibrant and united place. It put the World Cup –

a competition of incomprehensible scale and significance back then – into thrilling and relatable context.

Pavarotti seemed to bellow the final victorious bars of *Nessun Dorma* every time I opened it. He didn't, obviously, because the technology to make that possible would have made the sticker album prohibitively expensive. Plus, I liked to study that album, past my allocated bedtime, by torchlight beneath my duvet. The sound of a fat Italian man bellowing would have probably alerted my parents in more ways than one.

The Italia 90 album may have broadened my horizons, but I didn't complete it. I *wanted* to see it disappear into my bedside drawer with every last Milla, Matthäus and Maldini neatly in place, but at the age of six – when it was hard enough to sit through an episode of *Transformers* without climbing or eating something – the chances of me spending weeks searching for Steve Hodge were slim.

For one thing, Steve Hodge was incapable of turning from a man into a truck. As far as I know, Steve Hodge is *still* incapable of turning from a man into so much as a hatchback. For another thing, I didn't even know what Steve Hodge looked like. So I never did find him. My first sticker book disappeared, first into the attic and then altogether, with dozens of orphaned names still inside.

But a seed had been sown. In the early 1990s, when tele-vised football was still a rare treat and trips to The Dell (my Southampton-supporting dad's choice) or Fratton Park (my dad-baiting home town preference) just as infrequent, sticker albums played an integral role in hot-housing my early fascination with football into a fully-flowered obsession. In those pre-historic pre-internet days, sticker books were miniature journeys of Zissouan discovery into the footballing depths.

Each empty page was an opportunity to learn more about the game. Without my albums, I would have dumbly travelled through my childhood not knowing the name of Roy Wegerle's first club[4], Gary McAllister's birthday[5] or Ryan Giggs's weight[6].

. . . .

4   The Tampa Bay Rowdies.
5   25 December 1964. He missed a penalty against England at Wembley *and* his birthday is on Christmas Day. So: crap at pens and only one lot of presents a year. No wonder he looks so miserable.
6   Sixty-eight kilos, or about ten stone. And most of that was chest hair and the expectations of the Welsh nation on his shoulders.

I might never have met Scott Sellars, Peter Fear or Nii Lamptey.

At school, the albums became focal points at the start of each new season. August may be the long-established start of the footballing calendar, but to a schoolboy hooked on collecting small photographs of men three times his age whom he had never met, each new campaign only truly began when your swaps pile did.

Unfortunately, swaps were always my particular area of expertise. My Pro Set doubles-pile was so heavy it made me walk with a limp when I put it in my coat pocket. My attempt at completing Panini's *Football 92* ended with a ~~mountain~~ quite big hill of left-over Ken Monkous, Trevor Peakes and Gordon Duries. A Clayton Blackmore-induced meltdown the following year – he appeared in packets so often I took out a restraining order against him – brought a similar end to my *Football 93* campaign. The restraining order wasn't granted, unfortunately. I still feel a pang of nerves whenever I'm in Wales, though.

It didn't stop there, either. My attempts at finishing Merlin's *Premier League 94* album, a book that included a superbly simian sticker of Richard Keys and an ambitious prediction Adie Mike would be a 'future Premier League star', crawled to a standstill under a weight of un-swappable Terry Fenwicks. Or to give him his full name that year, Terry Fenwick-Again.

And predictably enough, the story was the same the following season. My *Premier League 95* swaps pile grew so large, it became a third child in the Carroll-Smith household. My grandma knitted him a hat. Mum set him a place at the dinner table. Dad grounded him time and again for not eating his peas.

As in previous years, a fruitless spring followed a barren winter, and my *Premier League 95* album was still emptier than the DW Stadium on a League Cup night. It disappeared into the loft, never to be seen again. 'Sticky', my adoptive brother, left home shortly after. A flimsy, lightweight character, he is now a Conservative MP. We don't get along.

After five years, a pattern of consistent under-achievement had formed. My sticker collecting history was more chequered than a Croatian national team photo. Worse still, it felt as though I had become the Tottenham Hotspur of the sticker world: forever certain I was on the verge of success, but apparently destined to forever let it slip through my fingers.

Premier League 96 was published in November 1995. The album, as in previous years, was the must-have playground accessory. The same disorderly queue snaked from the newsagent's counter to the pavement outside, come sun, rain, sleet or snow. Every penny in my piggy bank ended up in a newsagent's till.

My opening ceremonies remained unchanged; still a mixture of feverish excitement and white-gloved, snooker ref delicacy. I drew the same exploratory line with my thumbnail across the top of each new packet. I tore into each with equal precision, unending expectation still tingling in my fingertips. Hope, as always, hinged on catching a glimpse of something shiny or elusive inside.

Experience told me not to expect too much. But that year, something was different. Instead of finding an infinite number of Steve Boulds[7] or enough Gary Pallisters to fill a (very repetitive, quite unhappy) Pallister family album, I got lucky. For once, my swaps pile did not overflow with dead-eyed Edinburghs, Impeys, Ruddocks or Fenwicks. Instead, I found stickers – shiny, elusive, both – with alarming regularity.

In fact, I found them all. Barry Venison, his peroxide Whitesnake mullet flowing; Steve Morrow, goateed and grumpy, like a postman with a hangover; David Beckham, centre-parted and pale, more Comet trainee than global icon; Colin Hendry, his craggy facial features in random, Picassoan arrangement. Each of them, and 526 others, found a happy home in my sticker album.

I bought well, traded intelligently, kept my slim squad of swaps well organised and had my fair share of luck. But in the end, there was no drama, no competition. I found the stickers I needed and I stuck them in. Which is a pretty good technique when it comes to sticker collecting.

In the end, the 1995/96 season was a story of simple sticker success. At long last, the ghosts of *Italia 90*, *Football 92* and *93*, and *Premier League 94* and *95* had been buried. No, slain, because there wouldn't be much point burying a ghost. On a sunny spring

......

7 An infinite number of Steve Boulds, left alone in a room for an infinite amount of time, will eventually arrange their typewriters into an infinite number of flat back fours.

afternoon in April 1996, I finally had tangible proof I was a true football obsessive, a real fan: *Premier League 96* was complete.

* * * * *

It was a sunny spring afternoon in April 2012. I was in the loft of my parents' house – for some reason, I forget why – a small torch clamped uncomfortably between my teeth, rummaging through an assortment of random rubbish.

Dozens of frail, fraying cardboard boxes were littered around the dark and musty attic. Ancient golf bags, loose Christmas decorations and tall towers of de-boxed videos jostled for dusty position.

After ten minutes of aimless rootling, I had managed to find little more than one box of old school books, one and a half pairs of Gray-Nicolls batting pads and two Sega Mega Drive controllers, sadly divorced from the console itself.

But in the box of school stuff, a yellow folder was peeking coquettishly out from beneath the lid. I pulled it out and saw that in one corner, in tentative pencil, was my name. Inside were reams of ancient English essays, maths papers and school reports. I read a few of the essays, 'What I Want To Be When I Grow Up' (option one, airport run taxi driver, so I could 'listen to the radio and take people on their holidays') and a report on Ted Hughes's *The Iron Man* which concluded, waspishly, that the book was '… only *quite* good, not *very* good'.

I read a few school reports too. In most, my timekeeping and organisational skills were called into question. It was reassuring to find out how little I had changed. I have long been notoriously disorganised and endlessly late for things. My sense of timing is usually closer to Emile Heskey than Pippo Inzaghi.

But at this particular moment, it was faultless. I was in the right place at the right time. A perfect storm of lateness and disarray had led me to this point. Because there, tucked behind so much crumbling juvenilia, was another book. A book with a shiny red cover. A book I hadn't seen for 16 years. A book with 'Premier League 96' written in large gold letters on the front. My sticker album, basically. I hope I'm making that clear.

Somehow, the album had survived countless spring cleans and boot sales. The pages were still relatively crisp and neat, still alive with colour and detail. The staples still stubbornly held the whole package together. I stared at it for a few moments, shocked and delighted to have found it after so long. The faces on the front cover – Barmby, Ginola, Redknapp (J, obviously) – were as youthful as ever.

I flicked the book open somewhere near the centre pages and a peculiar reunion with dozens of long-lost childhood friends (acquaintances really) began. Names and faces I had half-forgotten – Jason Lee, Noel Whelan, David Burrows – came rushing back. I marvelled at the rows of relentlessly normal, pleasingly war-torn players on show. I felt my heart leap with joy at seeing Wimbledon as a fully-fledged top-flight team. I chuckled at Barry Venison's still-hilarious hair metal mullet. I felt a pang of sadness to see a young Gary Speed.

But I was delighted to see my old album. It was everything I remembered, a perfect, amber-cast artefact from an era of such giddy excitement and simple promise. I flipped back to the opening page of the album and began working through it, cover-to-cover. It wasn't so much the neat and completed rows of stickers I was looking forward to, as the total absence of any of the tempting and empty spaces which had first drawn me into the world of football stickers.

But by page five, there was a problem. By page 127, there were half-a-dozen. Six stickers were missing.

And now the title of the book makes sense. Phew.

Jokes, 4–6.

Stern John, *n* – A toilet at the very back of a ship.

UEFA, *n.* – Horseshoe-shaped ice-cream garnish.

Steven and Gary Caldwell's ancestors; very proficient users of the telephone.

Two

I FELT AS though the wind had been punched from my chest. I checked and re-checked the album, convinced it was a trick of the dim attic light that had made those stickers vanish. But it wasn't. There was no magic, no foul play. The album was just incomplete.

In an instant, proud, conquering history was suddenly re-written as wrack and ruin. Not even John Beresford's haircut – a cross between regulation boy-band curtains and a Jana Novotna power quiff – could cheer me up. It made me laugh, obviously. Just less than it should have.

My first instinct was to squirrel the book away and pretend I had never found it. My second was to destroy it by controlled explosion. The first idea was stupid – I would have re-found the album at some point and been forced to go through this rigmarole all over again. The second idea required a sophisticated robot, and I didn't know any. I didn't *even* know an unsophisticated robot from a rough neighbourhood who might do the explosion on the cheap.

I made a list of the six players missing:

Stuart Ripley (Blackburn)
Lars Bohinen (Blackburn)
Philippe Albert (Newcastle)
Scott Minto (Chelsea)
Gary Penrice (Queens Park Rangers)
Keith Curle (Manchester City)

From memory, I knew my dirty half-dozen had played hundreds of top-flight games and won countless international caps. They had turned out for teams in Belgium, Norway, Portugal and Switzerland, winning league titles and losing cup finals along the way. They were probably quite an interesting bunch, and almost certainly a handy six-a-side team.

But they could have been anyone. To me, they were not six former Premier League footballers, but a silent, absent minority, a piddling 1.1 per cent spoiling it for the other 524 stickers, and spoiling it for me. I hated them all. I Googled 'how to perform a controlled explosion of a quite old sticker album in your own home'. There were no results.

Of my missing six, only Scott Minto and Keith Curle were still on my footballing radar. Keith, a veteran of ten clubs and three England caps[8], had remained in the game. He had managed Mansfield, Chester City and Torquay, worked as a coach and assistant manager under Neil Warnock at Crystal Palace and QPR, before returning to management with League 1 side Notts County. Scott had moved into the media after a career that took him from Charlton to Rotherham via Chelsea, Benfica and West Ham, and secured a job as lead anchor for Sky's La Liga coverage.

Sticker three, former Bristol Rovers, Watford, Aston Villa and Queens Park Rangers striker Gary Penrice, was now a respected scout working across Europe for a number of Premier League and Championship clubs. According to his Wikipedia page, 'Porno Penrice' (his nickname from his playing days) was a 'friendly and respected member' of his local community. I wondered if there was a link between the nickname and his popularity in the village, then crossed my fingers that there wasn't.

Lars Bohinen was living somewhere in Norway. I found him on Twitter and discovered startling pictures elsewhere on the web of the former Nottingham Forest and Derby County midfielder in a sparkly, figure-hugging shirt, cut to his navel. Thankfully, it turned out that as well as working as a football pundit on Norwegian television, Lars had appeared on the country's version of *Strictly*. Presumably, he only wore the spangly stuff for the dancing.

Best of all, I learned Lars had once boycotted an international match against France in protest at the French Army conducting

· · · · · · ·

8   That's three times as many as David Nugent, at the time of press. And probably long, long, long *after* the time of press too.

nuclear weapons tests in the South Pacific; proof you can't judge a book by its cover. Or the character of a former Premier League footballer by the photos of him in blue satin and sequins.

Sticker five, Philippe Albert – marauding, moustachioed star of the Premier League in the mid-1990s – had returned to his native Belgium and set himself up in the fruit and veg business. In some ways, it was a career move that made some sense. This, after all, was a man famous for spectacular chips (Rimshot).

But besides that interesting pip of information, there was nothing more to report. Philippe had no Twitter account, no website, and judging by recent pictures of him, no moustache anymore either.

The loss of his famous facial fuzz was particularly disappointing, as he had timed its removal terribly. In the trendier parts of Brighton and east London, you couldn't move for Albert-inspired moustaches. Philippe had been a hipster footballer before the concept of football hipsters even existed. And what could be more hipster than that? Marcelo Bielsa managing St Pauli, that's what.

That left Stuart Ripley, the former Middlesbrough, Black-burn, Southampton and England midfielder. Stuart had been busy since hanging up his boots, but he hadn't moved into coaching, scouting, punditry, ice dancing or even vegetables. He was travelling a road less travelled. Less travelled than vegetables, even. He had become a solicitor.

I quickly found his profile on the website of the law firm he worked for. After graduating from the University of Central Lancashire in 2007 with a degree in Law and French, Stuart had become a trainee at a firm in Manchester. Since then, he had become one of the country's leading specialists in football law. He had worked with the Football Association, the Premier and Football Leagues, and FIFA. And he spoke French. He made me feel quite bad about my own achievements.

Beneath his impressive biography was a link to his e-mail address. I hovered my cursor over it, clicked, and began typing out a message to him. It would be great if you could imagine the sound of typewriter keys now, to help set the scene. Sure, that's technically my job, but this way is just easier.

Hi Stuart,

My name is Adam Carroll-Smith. I'm a sports journalist based down on the south coast. I've written for tabloids and broadsheets for the last couple of years.

I just thought I would drop you a line because recently I discovered an old sticker album of mine. It's a Merlin Premier League 96 collection.

To cut a long story short, I thought I had completed it. But on closer inspection, it turns out I haven't. Six stickers are missing. Yours is one of them.

So, with that in mind - it would be great to meet for a chat ... and a quick photo for the album, maybe?

Thanks for your time,

Adam.

I checked it over once, twice, three times, then sent it. You can stop imagining the sound of typewriter keys now. With one click of a mouse (imagine the sound of a mouse clicking) and a few confident keyboard strokes (back to the keyboard sound), my mind had been made up. My big idea (imagine sound of light bulb turning on) had arrived.

I realised that this album could not be allowed to remain empty. Starting with Stuart, I would track down and photograph the six players missing from my album, use those pictures to make my own replacement stickers and bring *Premier League 96* to completion. It seemed the only logical thing to do. This is what is known in the story-telling trade as a 'pivotal moment'. They don't normally recommend you point it out, but I'm just being thorough.

Of course, I realised that I was being slightly erratic. I *should* have been able to throw the album back into the loft and forget all about it. It *shouldn't* have mattered that the book wasn't all I remembered it to be. But it did. Completing the book suddenly seemed like an urgent, pressing matter. I wasn't entirely certain why it felt so important, but I was convinced of one thing. This was a *great* plan.

(You can turn that light bulb off now.)

* * * * *

4 April 2012
Wednesday

'A great plan? No.'

'Yes it is. It's *great*. Like Operation Mincemeat, or the Trojan Horse.'

'Both great plans. But this … '

'This is as good, and much simpler. No subterfuge. No slaughter. No woodworking.'

'But why do you need to … '

'Because it's *incomplete*, Rosh. I need to *complete* the album *because* it's *incomplete*.'

'Stop saying everything in italics. It's annoying.'

'How can you tell?'

'*I just can.*'

'Really? I can't.'

'Clearly not. Anyway, can't you just buy the stickers?'

'No. The album is 16 years old. They don't make the stickers anymore. And buying them would be cheating.'

'Fine – get a photo of each of the players from the internet and stick them in.'

'Also cheating. And rubbish. And too easy.'

'Too easy?'

'It's a challenge, Rosh. If it was too easy, it wouldn't be a challenge. It would be a joke, a folly, a waste of time. The Scottish Premier League, basically.'

'Is that a football joke?'

'Since about 1988, yes.'

Rosh has been my friend for more than 15 years, in spite of one major obstacle to our friendship. He knows nothing about football. He reckons a Panenka is a kind of sweet Croatian pastry. He thinks Jürgen Klopp is the bassist in Rammstein. But somehow, we've made it work.

In recent months, however, something had changed. We had passed a point of no return. We had dived over a cliff edge, like a marginally more masculine Thelma and Louise, and crashed headlong into a strange and uneasy new phase of our friendship. Our relationship had ascended – or sunk perhaps, it was too early to say – to another level. After a little while as colleagues working for the same company, he had been promoted. He was now my boss, and as such, the undisputed senior partner in our friendship. His signature was on my pay cheques. He was my superior. The Puyol to my Pique.

And he was a changing man. In the past 12 months, Rosh had settled down with a new girlfriend in a new flat. He had joined a gym and started reading proper books instead of graphic novels. He owned tools, which he used for odd jobs, which he enjoyed doing. He had a Clubcard. He was an adult.

I, however, remained happily mired in adolescence. I hadn't moved into soft-shoed domesticity yet. I had joined a gym, but only to drink the complimentary juice and use the wi-fi to download *The Larry Sanders Show*. I was contemplating completing my old sticker album. That was pretty immature. I was a few months short of my 28th birthday but adulthood felt a little like listening to a football phone-in or paying to watch an England friendly; a perfectly sound idea in theory, but in practice, not much fun.

Rosh and I were sitting in his local in east London. The pub was empty, save for a few weathered regulars propped up by the bar. John Cale's '4'33"' played on the jukebox. Rosh was outlining precisely why he was opposed to my sticker album plan. He had pulled some favours to get me this new job. He had even promised to try and wangle it so I could work from home most of the time, and only come into the office for the occasional meeting. He was worried that I was about to let him down. He warned me that if I did, he would have to fire me with extreme prejudice.

I did my best to convince him I could manage my workload and complete my sticker album at the same time. He didn't believe me. Neither did I. The conversation ground to a sudden and bad-tempered halt, like Craig Bellamy pulling a hamstring. I don't do well with awkward silences. A police siren shrieked along the street outside, before dying away into the distance.

'That's the Doppler effect,' I said.

'What is?'

'When a sound changes pitch as it gets further away.'

Rosh picked up my sticker album: 'And what is it called when someone invests unnecessary significance in some ancient and shiny artefact they should have forgotten about decades ago?'

'Being an England supporter?' I said.

Nothing.

'Being an England supporter?'

Nothing.

'Being an England sup ... '

'Is that a football joke?'

'Off and on since about 1970, yes.'

The conversation eventually moved on. Our friend Jess arrived. She, like Rosh, holds no interest in football. I mentioned the name Jürgen Klopp and the word Panenka to her. She told me Jürgen was 'brilliant in *Inglorious Basterds*' but that, unfortunately, she's never been to Croatia. And she doesn't really enjoy sweet pastry.

Rosh and Jess sat and talked films and music and whatever else for a few minutes, but I was a passenger. Wherever their conversation headed, I found a way to drag it back to football and back to my album. I day-dreamed about Philippe, Stuart, Scott, Gary, Lars and Keith. I imagined meeting each of them and triumphantly pressing their smiling faces into my album. Not their actual faces. Photographs.

Jess left the table. She had agreed to meet a friend, also from our mutual home town of Portsmouth, who was staying up in London for a while. She spotted her queuing at the bar and rushed off to meet her. Rosh, in a transparent bid to avoid any further discussion about mid-1990s football stickers, made a phone call. I sat quietly flicking through the pages of *Premier League 96*.

Jess returned a few minutes later. Stood beside her was a girl with dark green hair and chestnut-brown eyes. Or the other way around. She smiled and introduced herself. Her name was Anna and she was beautiful; beautiful enough that I suddenly felt an overwhelming urge to hide *Premier League 96*.

Women like Anna – women unlike Anna too – are not drawn to men who carry their childhood sticker collections everywhere like a Linus blanket. Worse still, this was an album with pictures of David Ginola and Jamie Redknapp on the front. I didn't want to invite those sort of comparisons. Nicky Barmby, however, I felt I could take.

I subtly stole the album back into my bag and started talking with Anna. For the next few hours, we bonded over a shared love of *Arrested Development*, an identical love/hate relationship with gin, and a mutual belief Kermit the Frog was trapped in a violent and dysfunctional relationship with a karate-chopping whack-job, and that the saddest thing about *The Muppet Christmas Carol* was not the plight of Tiny Tim, but the fact Miss Piggy had somehow tricked Kermit into impregnating her.

Now, that's some pretty niche-interest stuff. Particularly the Kermit and Miss Piggy nonsense. I was instantly convinced she was someone pretty special.

As we talked and laughed together, I felt a sticky swell of fear and excitement tumble around my gut. It was an unusual but not unpleasant feeling. And it was strangely familiar too – it reminded me of something, and somewhere, I just couldn't think what, or where. It had definitely been a while since I had felt anything like it.

At the end of the night, I offered to walk Anna home to the flat where she was staying with a friend. She said yes. For a mile or so we walked and talked, and as we turned down her street, I plucked up the courage to ask for her number. She agreed.

I pulled my phone from my pocket and handed it to her. She typed in her number, but immediately seemed anxious to return my handset. She had touched something, she said, and something had popped up (not like that). I took back the phone, and saw that an e-mail was open. While Anna apologised profusely, I read it.

As soon as I saw what it was, and who it was from, I panicked. It was an e-mail I really, *really* didn't want Anna to see. I asked her if she had read the contents of the message. She said she hadn't seen anything. I asked her again. She looked as though she resented being asked twice. She promised she had seen nothing.

A second or two of awkward silence passed. I was panicking. I was horribly aware how suspiciously I was acting, how my jumpy reaction to a simple e-mail was quickly souring an excellent evening with Anna. In the near-distance, I heard a police car rush past, sirens blaring.

'That's the Doppler effect,' I said, for absolutely no discernible reason.

'Pardon?'

I missed the opportunity to say literally anything else – something idiotic or prejudiced would have done the job – and repeated myself. Anna looked at me blankly. I pressed on.

'The Doppler effect – it's when a sound changes pitch as it gets further away.'

'Right, well … '

'I think it also has something to do with rainfall.'

Anna smiled, cut me off with a hasty goodbye, and disappeared into her flat.

I started the long walk to catch my train back to Portsmouth. I spent a few minutes finding something appropriately gloomy to listen to on my iPod – some Interpol, maybe – but on my way to the Is, I got distracted in the Fs. I ended up dancing into Waterloo station to 'Big Love' by Fleetwood Mac, and feeling a lot more positive about how the night had ended with Anna as a result. Physical exercise and Lindsey Buckingham had convinced me that all was not lost.

Sure, I had acted a little oddly, but the situation was retrievable. In fact, I had done well to behave as calmly as I did, because when Anna handed me my phone and I saw the e-mail, my reaction might have been far, far worse.

I could have erupted into a fit of excited whooping (which would have invited questions) or curled up in a ball out of sheer embarrassment (which would have invited more). Because on the one hand, this e-mail was a cause for immediate celebration, proof that if you ask an unlikely question, sometimes you will get a thrilling and unexpected answer.

But on the other (hand), it was an e-mail that I absolutely did not want Anna to see. It was a potential source of great humiliation; an e-mail which proved that I was unequivocally not a man, but an immature man-child. I re-opened my e-mails.

> Adam,
>   You are incredibly lazy. But Mum says that, just this once, she will do your washing. Leave it in a bag in the garage. Do not bring it in the house.
>   No underwear.
>   Dad.

As you can see, this e-mail was, without question, a cause for immediate celebration. It was proof that if you ask an unlikely question, sometimes you really will get a thrilling and unexpected answer. It was, however, also an e-mail that I absolutely did not want Anna to see; an e-mail which was potentially a source of great humiliation, and one which proved that I was an immature man-child.

But this *wasn't* the e-mail that sent me into the early stages of a panic attack outside Anna's flat. This *wasn't* the e-mail Anna might have seen: I had clicked this one open by mistake. I closed it down – actually, I sent a quick reply re-negotiating the 'no underwear' part of the offer – and opened the e-mail that really had sent me into a frenzy of nerves.

> Hi Adam,
> I would be happy to help you out with your sticker collection.
> I can meet you next Wednesday, the 11th. Shall we say 12.30 at my office?
> Just out of interest - who are the other 5 players?
> Kind regards,
> Stuart Ripley.

Anna might have seen everything – including the passion-killing couplet 'sticker collection' – or she might not. If she had, she would probably never want to speak to me again.

But for now, I had more pressing concerns. This e-mail meant my sticker quest was officially underway. I had some planning to do. I mapped out my trip to Manchester immediately. The route looked straightforward enough. All I had to do was get in my car and drive due north (the opposite direction recommended by television Mounties) for about four hours.

I replied to Stuart, and accepted his invitation. And as I slipped into bed that night, tired and happy – like Craig Bellamy after six hours on an Alan Shearer-shaped punching bag – I allowed myself a quiet and triumphant little fist pump[9]. Sticker number one of six was in the bag. And so, despite dad's warning, were my underpants. I texted Anna, to tell her how nice it had been to meet her. She didn't reply.

. . . .
9   Not a euphemism.

Jokes, 7–9.

A (quite) erotic story: Glenn Helder and then, Glenn Roeder. Lucky girl.

Newell's Old Boys vs. Young Boys Bern: a game guaranteed to attract a *very* large police presence.

Which Dutch footballer always smells fantastic? Frank Rightguard.

Three

11 April 2012
Wednesday

I WAS IN Manchester. So too was Stuart Ripley. With any luck, we were, in fact, inside the same building: a solicitors' office not far from the train station.

A week had passed since the end of chapter two. Some other stuff – mostly administrative work and prolonged bouts of procrastination – had occurred in the previous seven days, but none of it really merits a paragraph to itself. I don't have words to just spunk away, I'm up against a word count, for goodness sake. But to give you an example: at one point during this week, I walked into my lounge and mistook an old, very deflated party balloon for a cat. I don't own a cat. It made me jump out of my skin. But that's not interesting, is it? Exactly. Let's push on.

Inside the quiet, pastel and pine lobby of Stuart's office, I introduced myself to the receptionist, a neat and tidy lady of about 40 (years). She asked me if I would like to take a seat while she called through to Stuart's desk. I thanked her for the generous offer, but told her I would just sit on one instead. She didn't laugh. I didn't blame her.

From my seat on the other side of the room, I listened as the receptionist – let's agree to call her Brenda – spoke quickly and quietly to a voice on the other end of the line. After a few seconds, she replaced the handset, and motioned me back towards the desk. Bad news, she said in a whisper: Mr Ripley was not answering his phone, which meant he was away from his desk. She asked if Mr Ripley was expecting me. I told her he was, and that I had an e-mail to prove it.

The receptionist nodded, and said she would try another couple of numbers. I re-took my seat, picked up a legal magazine and tried to pass the time by reading a few articles, but each was packed with more jumbled jargon and awkward acronyms than an André Villas-Boas tactics dossier. After a while, I just looked at the pictures. Just like most of his Chelsea squad did, presumably.

I waited a little while longer. A phalanx of anonymous and chatty pinstripes shot past, each carrying files and folders and having loud, important-sounding conversations about legal things. It was like a scene from Ally McBeal, only everyone was chunkier, in a nice way.

Brenda stood up and waved me back. I leapt up, almost sending a potted plant spilling on to the carpet, and bounded towards the front desk.

'Found him?'

'Unfortunately not, no.'

'Oh.'

'Yes.'

'Right, well, do you know where he is?'

'Mr Ripley is out of the office on meetings all afternoon.'

I made an involuntary and very weird noise. It was a visceral expression of disappointment and surprise. I can't describe it. Which is unfortunate, given the nature of the medium I'm working in. Finally, I said something:

'In meetings, you say?'

'Yes, sir.'

'All afternoon, you say?' I wasn't sure, even as I was saying it, what this 'you say?' business was about.

'Yes, sir.'

'Are *we* sure?' I said 'we' in the hope that it might make the receptionist feel as though she and I were suddenly part of a team – the Team To Track Down Stuart Ripley (TTTDSR) – whose sole purpose was to locate elusive former Blackburn Rovers wingers.

'I'm afraid so,' she said.

I frowned. I was disappointed at the lack of enthusiasm I was getting from the other 50 per cent of my newly-formed gang. Maybe it was the name.

I told the receptionist I would wait a little longer. Sometimes, I told her, life throws up these temporary misunderstandings.

Michael Ricketts was mistakenly awarded an England cap once, I said, and that soon worked itself out. This could well be one of those times.

I sat down for a few more minutes, until a thought occurred to me. I hurried back to the front desk, almost knocking the pot plant over again.

'How many Stuart Ripleys do we have working here?' I asked, adverbially. I was certain I had got to the bottom of the mystery of the missing Stuart.

'One.'

'And he's ... '

'Busy in meetings, yes sir.'

'For the ... '

'Whole of the afternoon, yes sir.'

'Oh well. Still: the TTTDSR will fight on, won't we?'

'Pardon?'

'Nothing.'

I tried to look unmoved by the bad news, but I felt my face form into a doughy, babyish scowl. I slumped off and took my third impatient seat of the day. I listened as some atmospheric, scene-setting rain pitter-pattered metronomically against the window behind me. I heard cars sighing slowly through puddles on the road below. Then I stopped listening to them, as it felt like I was wasting time and needlessly slowing the narrative with too much artless description.

Instead, I checked the e-mail from Stuart again, just in case I had arrived on the wrong date or at the incorrect time. But there had been no mix-up, no error in comprehension. Today was the day. This was the hour.

Streams more narrow-shouldered suits entered and exited, flashing dark blue and grey. None of them were Stuart Ripley. One of them did look an awful lot like Stig Inge Bjørnebye, but that was no use to me: I already had his sticker, number 86, sandwiched (platonically, I assume) between John Scales and Mark Wright. I took his picture anyway, just in case I needed a swap at a later date. He was very good about it. Particularly as he wasn't actually Stig Inge Bjørnebye.

Stuart was clearly busy. That couldn't be helped, and it certainly wasn't his fault – but neither was it mine, and right now,

I needed someone to point an accusing finger towards. I wrote an e-mail to the usual target of my aimless fury.

To: FIFA
From: Me
Dear FIFA,

I'm e-mailing you as I've had a particularly disappointing day so far. I've decided to blame you.

Specifically, I've decided to blame your chairman — is it chairman? It's something like that. Lord? Emperor? Count? — anyway, Mr Sepp Blatter, basically.

To cut a long story short, I was supposed to meet a former Premier League footballer today, but something has gone awry. It's not his fault: he's a busy man. He was being tremendously generous agreeing to meet me in the first place. But neither is it my fault. Ergo: It must be Count Blatter's fault.

As such, I expect you to reimburse me the cost of my petrol, my parking and my food (an M & S Simply Food salmon and cream cheese sandwich, and a smoothie).

I will accept payment by cheque, BACS transfer or in the form of a deciding vote on where the next World Cup is going to be held.[10]

Cheers,

Adam

P.S. Any chance you could do something about bringing the Cup Winners' Cup back?

I clicked send, packed up my things – knocking the pot plant over in the process – and left before anyone noticed the mess.

* * * * *

For some reason, as I trudged out of Stuart's office building, I thought back to the first time I watched Pompey lose. Unusually, it wasn't until my eighth or ninth visit to Fratton Park. I knew Pompey occasionally lost – I heard losses announced by the posh

· · · · · · ·

10 Front-runners are: Jurassic Park; Hoth; the warehouse where they recorded *Robot Wars*; Scotland. Ultimately, it'll come down to whichever is best prepared to host top-flight football. So, Hoth.

man who read the classifieds, or saw them printed in the papers the next day – but up until that moment, they simply did not lose on my watch.

It was an afternoon kick-off in the thick of winter of 1992. The floodlights were on, illuminating the thin, persistent rain which was falling and turning the Fratton Park pitch into a half-greasy, half-boggy mess. I forget who the opponents were. Harchester United, maybe.

The first half was memorably tedious and aggressively goalless. So goalless, in fact, that it made you doubt if scoring goals had ever been the point of football. Pompey hoofed it forward, the visitors hoofed it back. When the ball flew out of play and into the crowd, no-one rushed to return it. Instead, fans hugged it to their chests like a mother determined to keep her young safe from danger. I was bored and frozen. I eavesdropped on the conversations around me. I begged for chips. I read my programme. I stopped reading my programme and begged for chips again. I ended up eating my programme.

In the second half, Pompey went a goal down thanks to a horrific goalkeeping error. I have an image of a long-range shot bobbling tamely through the keeper's arms and trickling gently over the line. It probably isn't an accurate memory, more a gluey collage of similar incidents I have seen in the years since.

But still: being a goal down was, in itself, no cause for alarm. A familiar pattern, one I had seen a few times already, would emerge. After the initial flurry of aggression and disappointment would come the rousing rendition of 'Play Up Pompey' from all four corners. Then, a Pompey onslaught on the opposition goal. And finally, the inevitable, run-preserving equaliser.

But a Pompey goal would not come. There was no onslaught, no endless pressure on the opposition area. As the match clock ticked into the final five minutes, I watched the tiny pocket of travelling fans celebrating in the windswept and uncovered away enclosure. I listened as their noisy chanting ricocheted happily around the ground, unchecked by any retaliatory racket from the home fans.

I was still finishing my programme, so my mouth was too full for me to be singing anything. But everyone else in the ground was quiet for a different reason. From the normally groaning rows around me, there were no tears, no complaints. Defeat, to everyone bar the pre-pubescent me, was simply a part of football. It was a lesson I had now learned, too.

My family and I left the game a few minutes early. They wanted to beat the traffic and I wanted to escape the cheers from the away end. I sulked all the whole way home, utterly unhappy in defeat and desperate, in my childish way, for some consolatory prize. We didn't even beat the traffic.

Back in present-day Manchester, I turned on my sat-nav.[11] The Homer Simpson voice I had installed especially for the journey told me to 'turn around', very loudly. He did it once every few seconds. Eventually, I got the message. I turned the key in the ignition and put the car into reverse. I felt genuine, stomach-churning disappointment that the day had not panned out as hoped. I had travelled hundreds of miles across the country in the last few hours, but I felt as though I had travelled back in time too. I was, once again, sat sulking in a car, utterly unhappy in defeat, eager to beat the traffic home.

As I inched my car out of the parking space, my phone vibrated in my pocket. It was a number I didn't recognise.

Adam:
'Hello, Adam speaking.'
Caller:
'Hello?'
The line was terrible. I could barely hear the person at the other end.
Adam:
'Hello? This is Ad…'
Homer Simpson:
[shouting]
'Turn around!!'
Caller:
'Pardon?'
Adam:
'Sorry, hi, this is Adam. Who is … ?'

. . . . . .

11 I had bought a sat-nav after my dad had told me my 'drive north for four hours' plan was 'imprecise'.

Caller:
'Hello?!'
Adam:
'Yes, hi, this is Adam, who is this?'
Homer Simpson:
[*shouting*]
'Turn around!!'
Caller:
'Adam?'
Adam:
'Hello! Yes, this is Adam! Stuart? Mr Ripley? Can you hear me?'
Caller:
[muffled]
'…hello…'
Homer Simpson:
[*shouting*]
'Turn around!!'
Adam:
'Are you free? Shall I come to the office now?'
Caller:
[*muffled, sounds like 'yeah, you pale warrior'*]
Homer Simpson:
[*shouting*]
'Turn around!!'

Enough was enough. I dropped the phone in my lap, and thumped away at the malfunctioning sat-nav. I smashed it. I bashed it. I rained down hammer-blows on the piece of junk until finally, Homer Simpson fell silent. He was no more. Dead. I had succeeded where Frank Grimes Jr. had failed.

I picked up my phone. The caller had hung up, so I called the number back. No-one answered. But all of a sudden, I felt a wave of excitement sweep over me: Stuart had called. I popped the car back into its parking space, saved Stuart's number in my phone, hopped from the car and started running.

And then I ran and ran and ran.

And then I felt myself get a stitch.

And then I stopped and frowned and asked for directions.

And then I walked and walked and walked.

And then I stopped and sat and waited.

I was back in the reception area of Stuart's office. I had re-introduced myself to Brenda as 'one half of the TTTDSR' and she had looked confused. When I reminded her that she was the other half, she looked even more perplexed.

I told her I was back and willing to wait as long as necessary for my meeting with Stuart. She asked if I had knocked over the pot plant on my previous visit. I said no, and sat down.

As I did, I remembered I was in a solicitors' office. There are a few places where I'm absolutely certain that lying is a very bad idea – a police station, a court room, a relationship – and a solicitors' office was definitely on that list too. I went back to the front desk and apologised for fibbing. She decided not to press charges.

And then, it happened.

A man – six feet tall, broad, brawny, familiar somehow, with a strong jaw covered in fashionable stubble – strolled over.

Unfortunately, it wasn't Stuart Ripley. This man's name was Ian or Mark or Bruce. Something like that. He just wanted to ask me what I was doing there, and if he could help. I told him I was waiting for Stuart Ripley. He nodded. Then he pointed at the pot plant to my right. 'Careful near that,' he said. 'Some idiot knocked it over earlier.'

And then it *really* happened.

Another man – six feet tall, broad, brawny, familiar somehow; with a strong jaw covered in fashionable stubble – strolled over.

We shook hands and he introduced himself. Sticker number 23 from page five of Merlin's *Premier League* 96 album, an absent 17 per cent (almost) of my album had materialised in front of me. It was Stuart Ripley. I do hope I'm making that clear. I told him I was here to take his picture. He nodded, and unlike Ian or Mark or Bruce he *didn't* point at the pot plant and imply I was the sort of idiot who might knock it over.[12]

· · · · · · ·

12 At this point, I must admit something. There was no Ian or Mark or Bruce. Ian (or Mark or Bruce) does not exist. He (they) was (were) a little ~~trick~~ illusion inserted to temporarily delay, for dramatic effect, Stuart's arrival. Sorry about that. I'm an unreliable narrator. Like Patrick Bateman in *American Psycho*, only with better taste in music.

Stuart suggested we head out of the office for a coffee, and I agreed enthusiastically. A little too enthusiastically, actually. I was nervous and gabbling. In a breathless few seconds, I apologised to Stuart for my poor phone reception, and told him about the pot plant 'incident'. I might have even called it a 'disaster'. He looked a little nonplussed and said nothing. I took a deep breath and stopped talking.

As we made our way towards the exit, I passed Brenda at her desk. I nodded a little nod of appreciation, and mouthed the words 'victory for the TTTDSR!' She looked blankly at me. I made a mental note to review her membership. And the name. Maybe the name was the problem.

* * * * *

Stuart and I headed out into the muggy Manchester air and across the road to the cafe inside the pretty Royal Exchange theatre. As we sat down at our table, I explained why I had travelled half the length of the country that morning. Stuart nodded along as I told him, face-to-face, what I had told him on e-mail. If he thought my motives and goals were peculiar, he was too kind to say so. I hoped the remaining five players would be as understanding.

For the past week, I had been reading up on Stuart. A Middlesbrough boy by birth, he had made his debut for the club in 1985, aged just 17. Over the next seven seasons, he had established himself as a young talent with a bright future, winning eight England Under-21 caps along the way.

After helping Boro gain promotion to the newly-formed Premier League at the end of the 1991/92 season, he joined big-spending Blackburn Rovers in the summer of 1992 for £1.3m – a figure which briefly made him the club's record signing until later that summer, when future human insomnia remedy and European football expert Alan Shearer signed from Southampton.

In 1993, Stuart won his first England cap in the final game of England's unsuccessful World Cup 94 qualifying campaign. A year later he played a vital role as Blackburn, bankrolled by Jack Walker's millions, won the Premier League title. In 1997, he won his second and final England cap and in 2002, after spells with

Southampton, Barnsley and Sheffield Wednesday, he retired at the age of 35.

Now, after a brief flirtation with physiotherapy, the multi-talented Mr Ripley was working as a solicitor.

All of which was perfectly interesting. But trivia and statistics aside, I soon realised I was hideously ill-prepared for this meeting. All I really wanted was a photo, but it seemed strangely inappropriate – somehow ungrateful, even wasteful – to just ask Stuart to pose for a picture and then be on my way back to the south coast.

Sat opposite me, chomping happily on a chocolate brownie, was a former England international who had made time in his busy day to see me. I told myself I should, at the very least, talk some football with him.

So we did. We talked about that year's Premier League title race and the form and fortunes of his old clubs. We talked about his life as a footballer in the glamour-free and penniless 1980s, and the ongoing state of the gilded and gaudy modern game. We talked debt and scandal, tactics and turnover, bonuses and Bentleys. For the 20 minutes Stuart had set aside in his busy schedule, we chatted merrily about the past, the present and the future of football in Britain, and how so much had changed, so quickly.

It was tremendous fun. Stuart was knowledgeable and passionate about the game, and a bright, engaging, fiercely intelligent person. I might have found myself sat opposite him largely by accident, but I was glad to have met him. But for now, our time was up. Stuart had work to do. I didn't, but I pretended that I did.

There was, of course, one thing left to do. I asked Stuart if he was ready for his close-up, immediately regretted my choice of words, and then fumbled awkwardly in my bag for my camera.

He said he was ready. But before he would pose up, there was one condition, one ground rule, to which I would have to agree before I took the photo.

'No cheesy grins,' he said.

STUART RIPLEY

As you can see, I managed to make him break his own rule, and coaxed a smile out of him. And no, I'm not joking. Sure, at first glance it *does* look like a scowl. But it's not. Look closely. That *is* a smile. A small one, sure, and definitely not a cheesy grin, but it's a smile all the same. It's there, just around the corners of the mouth; an enigmatic little half-smile creeping on in. Like the Teesside Mona Lisa. The Moouuerna Leeesa.

* * * * *

As I drove back to Portsmouth, I reflected on a long and busy day. And for the first time, I started to ask myself *why* I was so keen to complete this album; about why I felt so compelled to place this little quest at the top of my priorities when so many other things – my career, my love life, to name two – should surely be taking precedence.

But then, just a few minutes from home, that train of thought came to an abrupt halt. Another number I didn't recognise flashed up on my screen. I answered it. And when I realised who was calling, I nearly swerved off the road in excitement.

Belgium was calling.

One of them, anyway.

That's right.

Him.

Art, 1.

CATENACCIO.

Four

BUT NO, of course not. Belgium wasn't calling. How *could* it be Philippe Albert? There is just no chance that it would be. It's only chapter four.

Look how much of this book is left, for a start. I have no idea where he is. He doesn't know I exist. For him to call now would be preposterous.

Me:
'Hello?'
Caller:
'Hi, Adam?'
Me:
'Philippe?! Philippe Albert?'
I thought it best to check anyway.
Caller:
'Er ...what?'
Not Philippe, then.
Me:
'Sorry about that. Who's calling?'
Caller:
'Anna.'
Me:
[*stunned silence*][13]

• • • • • • •
13 Like normal silence, only 40% longer.

This was somehow more surprising than if it had been Philippe Albert. She had been ignoring my texts, so if this really *was* Anna, then this was very exciting news. I checked.

> **Me:**
> 'Anna?'
> **Anna (maybe):**
> 'Yes.'
> **Me:**
> 'Really?'
> **Anna (still only maybe at this point):**
> 'Yes.'
> **Me:**
> 'Wow.'
> **Anna (confirmed):**
> 'Hi ...'

It really *was* Anna. This *was* very exciting news.

I began to sweat. A lot. Think Jan Mølby chasing Aaron Lennon for an hour. Then imagine Jan is carrying Neil Shipperley on his back the whole time. Now imagine that Neil is carrying a six-feet-tall bucket of chicken. And now picture for me, if you can, that sat cross-legged inside that bucket of chicken, chomping away on the greasy carcasses and throwing the bones over his shoulder like a Swedish Henry VIII, is a late-period Tomas Brolin. Just think how much poor Jan would be sweating lugging that around. That, give or take, is how sweaty I was. Hearing Anna's voice made my heart pound in my ears. I felt a bit sick.

Anna was calling to ask if I was free for a drink the following evening. She had been in London for a week, but now she was coming back home to the south coast. I tried to play it cool, like one of the great icons of coolness (James Dean, Ryan Gosling, Snoopy in shades) and pretended to be wracking my brains, trying to remember whether or not I had already made plans. I was keen to give Anna the impression that I was the sort of man with a busy social calendar. I read in an article that women like a man who is busy and in demand.

The charade didn't last long. I dropped the act the very instant I heard Anna beginning to lose interest in the idea. I told her I *was* free. Definitely free. Free like a mason. I read somewhere that women *also* like a man who is flexible and spontaneous (same article).

We set a time, picked a location, made some plans – the usual stuff you have to do when you arrange to meet someone. And then we said our goodbyes, and I celebrated as I raced the setting sun down the M3. I low-fived the car stereo on and dance-dance-dance-dance-danced to the radio, even though it was a Radio 4 documentary about wool. It didn't matter. I didn't care. I was happy. I danced away until a Keane song came on and the urge to move inexplicably left me.

As I got closer and closer to home, that same feeling I had felt the first evening I had met Anna returned to the pit of my stomach: a churning cocktail of nerves and excitement. I liked it. I had missed it. But I still couldn't pinpoint why it felt so familiar.

* * * * *

12 April 2012
Thursday

It was date night and I was crazy nervous. Willy-Beaman-throwing-up-on-the-gridiron nervous. Anyone-English-taking-a-penalty nervous. [Name redacted]-in-court-on-[redacted]-charges. Anti-calm, basically.

I was early, so I took a seat on my own near the door. The bar itself was like a million others. You know what bars are like. There were men there. Women too. They were all talking and laughing. When they weren't doing that, they were pouring drinks into the lowest hole in their heads. Some music was playing, and it smelt like booze. The bar, not the music; the music didn't smell like anything.

If you're really struggling to visualise it, it was exactly like the bar in *Cheers*. For argument's sake, let's say it *was* the bar in *Cheers*. Ted Danson was working, and he gave me a free whisky to settle my nerves. 'Cheers!' I said. We laughed for about ten hours and he told me I was nearly as funny as Woody Harrelson.

I had made absolutely no preparations for the date. The fact that Anna had finally got in touch suggested she hadn't seen the e-mail from Stuart Ripley. If she had, she probably wouldn't have bothered to get in touch. I reasoned, therefore, that it would probably be best for me to make no mention of the e-mail incident that had so nearly spoiled our first meeting. Tonight was a chance at a fresh start.

Anna walked in, spotted me at the bar and walked over. Ted Danson brought over a white wine spritzer, entirely without prompting, which I thought was a little sexist.

'Hi,' she said, happily picking up her spritzer. That Ted Danson sure knows women, I thought to myself.

'Hi,' I replied.

'So, how have you been?'

'Pretty good. You?'

'Oh …pretty, pretty, *pretty* good.'

'Ha. Larry David.'

Anna gasped theatrically, 'Where?'

'America, probably.'

And then we both laughed.

You see what I mean about a connection, right? That, on paper, isn't a hilarious exchange. I can see that, now that I've actually written it on some paper. If you've never watched *Curb Your Enthusiasm*, it probably doesn't mean much to you.

But for Anna and I, it was proof of an instant bond. And that was exciting. Anna was *definitely* someone pretty remarkable. A brief lull, the sort that always seems to come after a period of slightly hysterical laughter, fell on the conversation.

'So,' said Anna suddenly. 'Who is he?'

I had no idea what she was talking about.

'Ted Danson? He's just a figment of my imagination.'

'No, come on! Who is *he* …' Anna asked.

'Who is *who*?'

An evil smile spread across Anna's face.

And then she said it:

'Who is Stuart Ripley?'

I made a noise that sounded very much like this – '…*ablurggggghhhhwhaaaaaahuhhhhhhummmmmm-well, listenerr-rrrummmmmahhhhhh…*' – for a few minutes, while I tried to formulate a strategy. For some reason, I felt an overwhelming urge to start telling her about the Doppler effect, but I stopped myself.

I'd been doing that too often recently.

I did some quick mental calculations.

I *could* lie.

I *could* concoct an inane and hopefully diverting little story about who Stuart Ripley was – an old school friend who was now a blimp salesman, maybe? – and Anna would never know about my sticker album.

But what if she had seen more of the e-mail than I had first thought? What if she had seen the words 'sticker album'? What if she had gone home and Googled 'Stuart Ripley' and worked out what I was up to? She would know I was a liar, and I read somewhere that women do not like liars (same article again, it was pretty long).

'So you *did* see the e-mail?' I asked.

'Only the name. But I'm curious now. It made you act *very* strangely.'

'He's an old school friend.'

'Yeah?'

'Yes. He sells blimps.'

'Blimps?'

'Blimps. Well, blimps *and* rigid airships.'

'Like the *Hindenburg*?!'

'Sure.'

'How's business?'

'Slow,' I nodded. 'Pretty slow.'

Anna frowned. 'That's weird. I thought it might have been the former Blackburn Rovers winger who won two England caps.'

Damn, I thought. I was busted, but I still had a choice to make – Anna knew I was e-mailing *the* Stuart Ripley, but she didn't know why. I could still rescue the situation. But I didn't care any more. I wanted to tell Anna the truth. So I did.

'Ah. Right. Yes. It is him.'

'So he's got two England caps *and* he's a blimp salesman? Impressive.'

'I was lying about the other bit.'

And with that, I decided to tell Anna the whole story. Anna would have to discover I was an immature man-boy. She would know that I *still* owned a sticker collection from the mid-1990s and worse still, that I was *still* trying to finish it. Like Howard

Webb chucking a yellow card into a tornado, I threw caution to the wind. I clicked open my e-mails, and handed Anna the phone. I told her to read the whole message this time.

Anna took the handset, and began to read. She immediately broke out into a broad grin, then clasped her hand to her mouth and stifled giggles. I felt my cheeks – face cheeks, come on – burn bright red with embarrassment.

'Your mum still does your washing?!'

The wrong e-mail.

Again.

I grabbed for the phone. Anna held it out of reach.

'And *no underwear*?' said Anna. 'Why *no underwear*?!'

I didn't answer, mainly because I didn't know why my mum wouldn't wash my underwear either. I told Anna to click through to the next e-mail, the one from Stuart.

For a minute or two, she read it. Her face remained expressionless throughout. She finished reading and handed me back the phone.

'So,' she said. 'Did you go?'

I nodded.

'And you got his picture?'

Nod number two.

'Can I see it?'

I nodded, for the hat-trick. I pulled a copy of Stuart's picture from my wallet – oh right, I should have mentioned earlier that I had made a small copy of Stu's picture and was now carrying it around in my wallet, like he was my wife[14] – and Anna looked at it closely.

'Why is he angry?'

'He's not. He's smiling.'

'That is a scowl.'

'No. It's a Mona Lisa smile.'

'A terrible Julia Roberts movie?'

'No, look: just around the eyes, and around the corners of his mouth. He's happy. At the very least, he's enigmatic. Just like the Mona Lisa. He's a Da Vinci.'

· · · · · · ·

14 Which he is not.

Anna grabbed a pen from her bag, and drew a curly moustache on Stuart's face.

'Well now,' she said, handing the picture back, 'he's a Salvador Dali.'

I checked later and discovered Salvador Dali was an artist famous for this sort of thing and not, as I first thought, the Bari manager who signed David Platt.

I told Anna to keep the picture as a 'first date' gift. She said flowers were more traditional, but we both agreed a picture of a scowling/smiling former Middlesbrough midfielder with a biro moustache was more original. She popped Stuart's picture in her wallet, like Stuart was her husband[15], and looked genuinely pleased as she did so. This, I decided immediately, was yet more evidence – not that I needed it – that Anna was a keeper. And not in the way Dino Zoff is a keeper. A keeper in the romantic sense of the word.

She was also, impossibly enough, interested in hearing *more* about my sticker album. News of my trip to see Stuart only seemed to stimulate her interest. Now, Anna wanted to know the names of my other absent stickers. She wanted to know all about how my attempts to reach the other missing five were going.

So I told her. I told her how, in the days following my trip to see Stuart, I had been on a happy but ultimately unsuccessful rampage: e-mailing, tweeting and telephoning all and sundry in the hope of finding Keith, Scott, Lars, Gary or Philippe.

Notts County's genuinely excellent and helpful press officer, Ralph Shepherd, had promised to pass my e-mail to Keith Curle once the season was over, but unfortunately – for me at least – the Magpies were right in the thick of the League 1 play-off picture. It might be more than a month before their season ended and Keith felt like posing up for me. I would have to stay patient.

The news was the same elsewhere. A few e-mails and telephone calls to Sky's press office had failed to bring me any closer to meeting Scott Minto. A flurry of tweets to Lars Bohinen had all gone unreturned, so too e-mails to his former clubs in England and abroad. Ditto for Gary Penrice and any of his former clubs. Philippe Albert was even further off my radar. Nobody seemed

• • • • • • •

15 Which he is not.

50

to have any idea where he was, nor how to reach him. He was nowhere. Well, Belgium.

Anna seemed excited by the whole pursuit. She didn't seem to think it was a preposterous waste of time. She wanted to know what my next moves would be, and how she could help me succeed in my quest. The only thing she didn't want to know was *why* I was doing all this. It was just as well she didn't ask. I still wasn't sure. The spaces were empty. They needed filling. That was all I had, so far.

* * * * *

The rest of the evening went very well. Anna and I swapped opinions on *Parks and Recreation,* suggested possible *Downton Abbey* spin-off series[16], and questioned whether England would ever produce a creative, play-making defensive midfielder like Andrea Pirlo or just keep slotting solid but unimaginative cloggers like Gareth Barry into that role[17]. It was fun.

At the end of the night, I offered to walk Anna home. She said yes. As we made it to her door, I asked her if she was free again in the next few days. She said yes. I suggested dinner on Saturday night. Anna accepted. And then we kissed goodnight. It was pretty brilliant. I have never scored at Wembley, but this was better. When you score at Wembley, only half of the people there are happy. The other half are disappointed. That is how goals work. But kissing Anna made literally 100 per cent of the people involved feel excellent.

As we wrapped up all that mucky business, Anna said something utterly unexpected.

'See you Saturday,' she said. 'Bring your sticker album.'

'What?! Why?' I asked.

'Because I want to see it. I'm curious. And find out why your mum won't wash your underwear too.'

I promised to do at least one of those things. Probably just the latter.

16 Me, '*Downton Flabby*; a show where overweight people slim down by helping Hugh Bonneville into his trousers.' Anna, '*Downton Wasabi*; a shot-for-shot remake of the original show, but everyone's peas are spicier.'

17 Me, 'Probably the former. What do you think?' Anna, '*Downton Stabby*? Tarantino could direct. Edith and Mary could have a musket fight.'

* * * * *

14 April 2012
Saturday

In the end, I barely did either. I *obviously* decided to leave my sticker album at home. I was worried I might leave it in the restaurant, or that in all the excitement of showing it to Anna, I might spill red wine across the Coventry City pages and leave David Burrows's pale little rabbit-like face stained bright red for ever more. I was also a little concerned I might not be able to relax and enjoy myself with Nicky Barmby's sad and beady little eyes staring at me. Worst of all, Anna might have been joking.

I met Anna outside her flat, and she immediately noticed I was empty-handed. She looked disappointed.

'No sticker album then,' she said. 'So what's the story with the underwear boycott then?'

'Personal reasons, apparently.'

'Personal reasons?'

'She wouldn't elaborate.'

Anna laughed. I pretended I was joking.

We started the short walk to the restaurant. After a few steps, Anna insisted the next time we met, I *had* to bring the sticker album. I seized on my opportunity and secured a third date before the second one had even started. The following Friday, I would take Anna out again, and this time, I would ensure *Premier League 96* came along for the ride.

Amazingly, the evening only got better from there. In the days since our first date, Anna told me she had been busy. She had, she announced proudly, been doing some very intensive Googling. She had been learning a great deal about the small band of former professional footballers I was so keen on meeting.

'Number one – Keith Curle,' she said. 'Manchester City. England. Now the manager of Notts County.'

'Very good,' I said.

'Number two – Scott Minto. Chelsea. Looks like he should be in Blue. Or A1. Or Another Level.'

'Did you know Another Level's debut single featured a rap from Jay-Z?'

'No, I didn't. Downhill from there for them, I guess,' said Anna. 'But *why* do you know that?'

'Not sure.'

'Would you like me to move on?'

'Yes.'

Anna chuckled, 'Number three is Gary Penrice. He has a moustache. I can't remember who he played for.'

'QPR, Watford, Bristol Rovers. Number four?'

'Lars Bohinen. Blackburn Rangers.'

'Rovers.'

'That *can't* be important,' replied Anna. 'He's Norwegian.'

'And our final footballer ...?'

'... is my favourite. Philippe Albert. He has a moustache too. A *brilliant* moustache. A Ron Swanson moustache. He played for Newcastle, he scored a goal against Man United and, as far as I can tell from my Google image search, has never smiled. Also like Ron Swanson.'

'Very impressive knowledge,' I said. 'You now know as much about football as Alan Shearer.'

'Is that a football joke?'

'Only since he became a pundit.'

Anna had really done her homework. She was beautiful, intelligent *and* she was interested in my silly little sticker album quest. That was a full house.

'That reminds me,' she said. 'Philippe also works as a football pundit on Belgian television from time to time. He is now my favourite Belgian. He's displaced Jean Claude Van-Damme from top spot.'

I told Anna the hyphen should *actually* go between the 'Jean' and the 'Claude', not the 'Van' and 'Damme'. She apologised for the error, then asked me how I could tell that she had said it incorrectly. I told her I wasn't sure, but that my friend Rosh could tell when people were talking in italics.

'*Can he*? Me *too*!' she said.

I sighed: 'I can't.'

'*Really*? But it's *easy* ...'

'Not for me.'

'Clearly. Anyway, I have something for you. I was going to wait until the end of the evening, but ...'

She reached into her bag and pulled out a small piece of paper, neatly folded down to the size of a business card. She handed it to me.

'What's this?' I asked.

'It's an address.'

I looked at it. It didn't look familiar. It looked foreign. Belgian, to be precise. It couldn't be, could it? Before I could ask, Anna smiled and confirmed it. Apparently it *could*.

'It's Jean Claude Van-Damme's – sorry, *Jean-Claude* Van Damme's – address,' she said.

'Oh. I thought it might have been ...'

'No, of course it's not. What would anyone ever have Jean-Claude Van Damme's address for?'

'*Personal reasons?*'

'Excellent call-back,' Anna replied.

'Thanks.'

'But seriously: it's not Jean-Claude's. It's Philippe Albert's.'

And then my jaw hit the floor. Which was pretty painful, seeing as it had to go through the table and my chair to get there.

Jokes, 10–12.

Phil Masinga, *n.* What the cameramen on *Top of the Pops* used to do.

Football philosophy 101: Thorsten Fink. Therefore, Thorsten am.

'Oh dear. That close-range shot has hit Ferdinand and he looks to be in some pain.'

[Football commentary | Football commentator describing the start of the First World War.]

Five

'Well,' said Anna, attempting to dampen my expectations, 'it's *a* Philippe Albert.'

'So it might not be the *actual* one?'

'Well, no.'

'Oh. Right. No. Of course not.'

'But ...'

'But?'

'But I think it is. Because I found something ...'

I raised my eyebrows and waited for Anna to continue.

'... Well, I Googled "Philippe Albert + his home + Belgium' ..."'

'Clever.'

'Thanks. Did you not think to try that?'

'No. But then I'm not very thorough.'

'Well anyway, what came up when I Googled all that was an article on a website. A Belgian football website. A Belgian football website written by an Englishman called John Chapman. Who fortunately enough, writes in English too, which is a bonus.'

I urged Anna on.

'Well, he interviewed Philippe Albert a little while ago. He wrote about meeting him. He wrote about going to Philippe Albert's house. And he wrote about exactly *which* town that house was in.'

I made a 'wow, that's quite some revelation!' face. Anna picked up her phone and began typing frantically. After 30 seconds or so, she had found what she was looking for. She tip-tapped her fingers on the table while she waited for the website to load. Then she thrust the phone into my hand and told me to read.

On the very end of the second line of the piece, John Chapman – whose website, www.belgofoot.be, is brilliant and very informative, albeit in ways he probably didn't intend – had written the words 'Wanfercée-Baulet'.

That, he wrote, was where he had met Philippe. I looked back at the slip of paper Anna had handed me earlier. At the foot of the address was the same hyphenated town name (the Belgians clearly love a hyphen).

Anna explained, sounding a little like a much prettier Chloe from 24, that once she had found the name of the town where Philippe lived, she had Googled 'Belgium residential listings' and found www.whitepages.be, a website where you could search for Belgian telephone numbers and addresses. She had punched in 'Philippe Albert' and 'Wanfercée-Baulet' and two addresses had popped up. One, for an F. Albert and a second for a P. Albert.

It had to be him, I thought to myself. The P. Albert one, obviously.

'It *has* to be him,' said Anna, apparently reading my mind. 'The P. Albert one, obviously,' she added, apparently doing it again.

'Doesn't it though? It must be.'

Anna nodded: 'There can't be two P. Alberts in such a small place, can there?'

'Probably not,' I said. 'There's more chance of Roy Hodgson singing "Face Down Ass Up" at the FA's Christmas party than there being two P. Alberts in the same village.'

'Is that a football joke?'

'The FA? Only most of the time.'

'Well,' said Anna, dragging the conversation back on topic, 'if you want to be certain it's the real Philippe, we could call him.'

'Could we?!'

'That number at the bottom is his home number. It was on the website.'

'We need the code for Belgium, and ...'

'No need. The number I've written down is the number you have to dial from a UK phone, including the Belgian code. Just don't call him now. They're an hour ahead. It's late.'

I thanked Anna for a solid five minutes, and told her this was the best date I had ever been on. She blushed, and warned me once more that it might not be the actual Philippe Albert.

I told her that it didn't matter either way. And it didn't. That she had gone to all this trouble was enough. This was the kind of awesome behaviour that makes a chap want to marry a lady. I made a mental note to try and do that with Anna one day.

* * * * *

16 April 2012
Monday

After a mildly hungover Sunday, it was time for the first day of my new job, working with/for Rosh. I had commuted from Portsmouth to somewhere that was technically London, but which no tourist would recognise as the capital.

But it was nice all the same. I had a big, fancy computer on my desk, there was a fridge full of free smoothies to my right, and to my left was a chap called Ed, who seemed very friendly. Within minutes of my arrival in the office he had waltzed over (figuratively) and offered me a pain au raisin, and a chai latte.

That was enough for me. Ed was now my friend. He was also, he was proud to tell me, something of an expert on Henry VIII. He knew everything there was to know about the fat old King, and invited me to test him. I asked for some time to formulate some questions and he agreed.

The more we spoke, the more certain I was that Ed was actually a 16th-century Earl – maybe the Earl of Chester – forced forward through time to live against his will in the 21st century, among all the skateboarding and calculators. But he was nice. I liked him. I felt certain he might become a central character in some hilarious adventures down the road.

For the first few hours, I got my head down (figuratively) and worked. Rosh would occasionally sashay out of his office, hand me some work to do, offer his opinion on how I should do it, then disappear back into his hidey-hole. I would spend a little while writing a piece of ad copy I thought was funny or punchy or clever, then Rosh would either green-light my work with the minimum of fuss and fanfare, or suck his teeth and say something vague and unhelpful, and send me back to my desk to re-work it.

But it wasn't all bad. I was guzzling my way through the smoothies like some fruit-starved sailor on shore leave to a stretch of shore with lots of fruit and juicing machines, and Ed had brought over two pain au chocolat[18] and another couple of chai lattes. He was now more like a brother to me – a brother who supplied me with pastry, and who knew that Henry VIII was born on 28 June 1491, the same year the Truce of Coldstream secured a five-year peace between Scotland and England, and Kanu turned 18.

Lunchtime arrived, as is the custom, in the middle of the working (and actual) day. Rosh disappeared (figuratively) into a meeting room, and Ed vanished (I'll stop now) from the building altogether. For a few minutes, I was alone in an almost entirely empty office, with nothing but the whir of a computer fan, the occasional chirrup of a phone and the gentle hum of a small refrigerator for company. I ate a sandwich at my desk. I was bored.

A little under 48 hours had passed since my date with Anna. Incredibly, I had resisted the urge to call Philippe. For now, his contact details remained safely tucked away in my wallet, beside a replacement picture of Stuart Ripley. Alone at my desk, I removed them both. I placed them on my desk and stared at them for a few seconds.

Meeting Stuart had been tremendously exciting. From the initial e-mail through the journey to Manchester, the agonising wait to see him and the eventual coffee, cake and conversation in the cafe, it had been a rewarding experience. Literally. I was now almost 17 per cent closer to completing *Premier League 96*.

I wanted more of that excitement. I wanted another 17 per cent. I picked up the phone and dialled, purposefully. I really went at the buttons, jabbing at the 0s and 3s and 6s like a man on a (phone-related) mission (involving a phone number with lots of 0s, 3s and 6s in it).

The call connected.

The phone rang for a few seconds.

I switched the phone from my left ear to my right.

Still ringing.

I switched it back to my right ear.

Still just ringing (the phone, not my ears).

Ring, ring.

. . . .

18 Like 'deer' or 'sheep', the plural of 'pain au chocolat' is simply 'pain au chocolat'. If you go into any decent patisserie and start asking for 'two pain au chocolats', they'll laugh you out of there. You'll be a joke in the world of pastry.

More rings than one of Bobby George's hands.
Ring, ring.
Or a well old oak.
Ring, ring.
Or Bobby's other hand. Also very ring-dense.
Ring, ring.
Nobody was answering. I hope I'm making that clear.
Ring …
'Hello?'
'What a dramatic development,' I thought to myself.
'Hi, my name is Adam Carroll-Smith,' I said, because it was true and I always try to be honest, at least while being honest is relatively easy.
'Hello, Adam.'
'Yes, hi. I'm just calling because – well, it's a bit complicated, actually – but I need your help. I'm trying to complete a very old football sticker album of mine, and your sticker happens to be one of the six that are still missing.'
'OK …'
'Yes, so, I'd really like to come and meet you – either in Belgium or in the UK if you happen to be over here at any point soon – and then take your photo, so I can fill your gap in my book.'
'OK.'
'Yeah. So how does that sound?'
There was a pause.
Quite a long one.
'I think it needs some work. You sound like a weirdo.'
'A weirdo?'
'A weirdo,' said Anna.[19] 'You sound nervous. But it was a good practice run, and we can work on what you'll say to Philippe Albert later. We'll work up a script. We'll do some practice calls. Come round at about seven. We'll call him at eight.'
'Yes. We'll call *the* Philippe Albert at eight.'
'We'll call *a* Philippe Albert.'
'*The*,' I said.
'*A*,' said Anna.

· · · · · · ·

19 Lose a turn if you thought I was calling Philippe Albert from my work line on the *first day* in a new job. Come on now. Use your head.

'The.'
'A.'
'The.'
'A.'
'Team.'
'Team?'
'Read it back.'
'The …A …Team? Oh.'
I gasped theatrically, 'Where?'
'America, probably,' replied Anna.
'Aren't they on the run though?'
'Yeah. In America, mainly.'
'But aren't they always in a jungle?'
'No.'
'So they're still in America, even though the government is after them?'
'Course they are. Because of Mr T.'
'Why?'
'He hates planes.'
'Ah, of course. He won't fly on one.'
'He doesn't even get *on* them.'

As mine and Anna's conversation drew to a close, I could feel a strange and unsettling warmth on my neck. I stopped listening to Anna – who was busy doing Mr T impressions by now anyway, and laughing at her own material – and slowly turned around.

I saw Ed standing directly behind me, arms folded, his face inches from mine. The warm and unpleasant breeze had been his breath. He had a large grin on his face – specifically on the lower third of it, between his nose and chin. With the early afternoon sun behind him, he looked quite creepy and imposing. Actually, *very* creepy. Creepier than a spider on tip toes, or Mark Lawrenson in drag. I ended the call with Anna and asked Ed how long he had been stood behind me.

'A while,' he said.
'Oh. Good,' I replied.
'Yeah.'
'What did you hear?'
'Nothing much.'
'Oh. Good.'

'Actually I heard everything. So, come on: explain …'

'Explain what?' I said, playing dumb – a role that was as much a stretch for me as the role of the neurotic, bumbling, New York-Jewish comedian Alvy Singer was for the neurotic, bumbling, New York-Jewish comedian Woody Allen in *Annie Hall*.

'Well, I'm very interested to hear why you're going to be giving the former Newcastle United centre-back Philippe Albert a call tonight.'

'Um, well …'

'And then when you're done explaining that, it would be really interesting to hear why you have a passport-sized photograph of Stuart Ripley on your desk, too.'

This was awkward. Rosh was already set against this idea. I had more-or-less promised I wouldn't mention my sticker album in the office. My only hope was that Ed wouldn't be interested, or better yet, that – like Rosh – he would think I was a complete idiot who was wasting his time on a very silly project.

I told Ed the whole story, regurgitating the choicest cuts of chapters one through four. He told me the story was a bit light on actual football and football stickers so far, but that he was interested.

He told me he had consistently failed to finish a sticker album, too. He had come close on a number of occasions, but there was always a sticker or two – 'an Oldham Athletic shiny one year; Stuart Nethercott, Kevin Gallen and a few others a year or two after that' – that remained uncollected. He thought he still had some old swaps in boxes at his parents' house and offered to bring a few in sometime soon.

Over his shoulder, out of the still-bright sun and through the office front door, came Rosh. I hurriedly told Ed not to mention our conversation to him. Under no circumstances, I reiterated at breakneck, John-Barnesian pace, was he to mention one word about this discussion. He nodded, silently. Though quite how he would have nodded noisily, I don't know. Looking at it, that's probably bad writing. The 'silently' could do with being deleted. I'll get it later.

Rosh, his eyes locked on his phone screen, passed wordlessly between Ed and I and disappeared into his office. He re-surfaced a few minutes later to tell me I could start working from home from Thursday. I celebrated with a smoothie. Later, Ed strolled over for a chat. He told me the mnemonic about Henry VIII's six wives – divorced, beheaded, died, divorced, beheaded, survived – was a lie. Henry didn't divorce any of them. The marriages were annulled.

I asked him if he had ever done any time-travelling, perhaps from the 16th century, or if he had ever been the Earl of Chester in a past life. He looked confused, then offered me another pastry.

* * * * *

I arrived at Anna's flat a few minutes before seven. She greeted me at the door and invited me inside.

Anna showed me through to her lounge, told me to take a seat, and offered me a drink. She disappeared from the room for a few seconds. When she returned, she was holding a bottle of beer in one hand, and a writing pad – one with yellow pages, the kind Sam and Josh used to write speeches on in *The West Wing* – in the other (hand).

'Some ideas,' she said, handing me the pad. 'And some Dutch courage,' she added, handing me the beer. The beer was American, but I didn't quibble. I looked at the pad.

1. Introduce yourself. Refer to yourself as a journalist. Tell him you're writing an article on retired footballers. Ask when you can visit him in Belgium. DON'T mention the sticker album.
2. Introduce yourself. Refer to yourself as an author and a journalist. Tell him you're going to be in Belgium a lot in the coming weeks, and you're writing an article. Ask when he might be free to meet. DON'T mention the sticker album.
3. Introduce yourself. Refer to yourself as a journalist, an author and a dedicated football sticker collector. Invite yourself to Belgium. Tell him EVERYTHING about your sticker album.
4. Blank.

Anna came into the lounge and sat beside me. She asked me what I thought of her ideas. I told her I was leaning towards options one and two. If I called Philippe Albert out of the blue and told him why I *really* wanted to meet him, he might run a mile. He might think I was an oddball. I told Anna it felt like a far safer bet to play it cool to begin with, then spring the sticker album nonsense on him once he was sat opposite me. She leaned forward, grabbed my bottle of beer and took a sip.

'Maybe,' she said.

'Maybe?'

'Yeah. Maybe. I prefer option three. It's bold.'

'It's risky. Be realistic.'

'No.'

'No?'

'No.'

'Fair enough. But isn't option three basically what I said to you on the phone earlier? You said I sounded weird. You said it needed work.'

'You did, and it does. But I've done some more research into Philippe Albert. He used to play for Newcastle, when Kenny Keegan was the manager. They played bold, high-risk football, right?'

'That's almost entirely correct.'

'So maybe he'll appreciate the bold, high-risk approach when it comes to this, too.'

I looked at Anna, my eyes wide with admiration. Before I could ask her how she suddenly knew so much about the cavalier character of the Newcastle United side of the Kevin – I decided not to pick her up on the 'Kenny' slip – Keegan era, she smiled, said the words 'YouTube' and 'Wikipedia', and took another sip from my beer.

Maybe Anna was right – perhaps Philippe really might appreciate a bit of honesty. Over the years, he must have had so many interview requests from journalists, all doubtless wanting to talk to him about the same things. Perhaps he would appreciate that I wanted to meet him for an entirely different, altogether more unusual reason.

Anna listened while I performed a dry run of my side of the conversation. It sounded OK.

Then I had another go.

Better.

And another.

Better still.

Anna checked the time. It was quarter to eight.

'Now,' she said, suddenly. 'Call him now. You're ready.'

I wasn't, but I did as I was told. I picked up my phone. I pulled the tatty scrap of paper Anna had handed me a few days earlier and typed in Philippe Albert's – *the, a,* I wasn't sure anymore – phone number.

I put the call on loudspeaker. A foreign dial tone sounded.

Boooooooop.

My palms were sweaty.

Boooooooop.

My brow? Also sweaty.

Boooooooop.

Top lip, ditto. I bet Philippe Albert's moustache was great for absorbing – or at least hiding – nervous top lip perspiration.

Boooooooop.

If only Richard Nixon had thought of that before his television debates with JFK, he might have won.

Boooooooop.

I picked up the pad and quickly scanned Anna's three options, 'Maybe one? Or two?'

Anna shook her head, 'Three. Be bold.'

Boooooooop.

I nodded, and composed myself.

Boooooooop.

Anna and I stared at each other, silent and anxious.

'He's not there,' I said.

'Let it ring.'

Boooooooop.

'He's not …'

'Let it *ring*.'

Boooooooop.

Boooooooo-click.

I put the phone down. Anna and I sat in silence for what seemed like an age. It was like a pause in a Harold Pinter play, only shorter and noisier. We could hear someone in the karaoke bar opposite singing 'How Long' by Ace. You don't get that with Pinter.

'Again?' said Anna.

'Again,' I replied.

I re-dialled and put the call on loudspeaker.

Boooooooop.

Nothing so far.

Boooooooop.

Anna crossed her index and middle fingers for luck.

Boooooooop.

The ones on the same hand.

Boooooooop.

Still nothing.

Boooooooop.

That was the 16th unanswered '*Boooooooop*' of the evening and I could take no more. Philippe Albert was not at home. Anna smiled sympathetically. She told me this was a temporary setback; we could try again the following night, and the night after that, until he answered. She picked up the pad, tucked it under her arm, then disappeared into the kitchen to get me a consolation beer.

Alone in Anna's front room, I began to wonder why I was doing this. Why was I so desperate to complete this long-forgotten and utterly unimportant sticker album? I had the chance to spend a lovely evening in the company of a girl I was steadily becoming ever-more smitten with, and I was spending it doing *this*?

Anna bounded back into the lounge. She wasn't holding any beer. She was, however, holding the notepad. She told me she'd had another idea. She thrust the pad under my nose. Number four wasn't blank anymore. I stared at the pad for a few seconds.

'You cannot be serious,' I *McEnroed*.

'I am,' replied Anna. She read option four aloud.

4.   Just show up at Philippe's house with your sticker album.

'But it's … *silly*,' I said, apparently without irony.

'No, it's a *great* plan.'

'Anna, Operation Mincemeat and the Trojan Horse were *great* plans. This is … '

'… as good and *much* easier. You won't need to trick any Nazis or build a wood horse.'

'Hopefully not.'

'You definitely won't. There aren't many Nazis about now, thank goodness. Or many Trojans.'

Jokes, 13–15.

Some Anagrams [20]

Rudi Völler = Lurid Löver (potentially libellous).

Alex Ferguson = Sex Fun Galore (happy retirement).

Sven Bender = Never Bends (ironic).

. . . .
20 I've just realised I miscounted the number of *booooooop*s earlier. I said it had taken 16 to make me finally hang up on Philippe, when it was actually 15. I owe you one. I'll drop it in somewhere later.

Six

ANNA WAS right about the Nazis and the Trojans.[21] But despite that, I was still not 100 per cent convinced by her plan. I asked her if I could borrow the pen and paper for a second or two. I had some tweaks to make to option four. I steadied the pad on my knees and began to write.

4. Just show up at Philippe's house with your sticker album. Learn the French for 'I'm sorry for this gross invasion of your privacy, Monsieur Albert. It was my girlfriend's idea.'

Anna looked at my embellishments, then snatched the pen and paper back. After a few rushed scribbles, she handed the pad back to me. More changes.

4. Just show up at Philippe's house with your sticker album. Learn the French for 'I'm sorry for this gross invasion of your privacy, Monsieur Albert. It was my girlfriend's idea.'
    Also learn the French for 'Your moustache is very impressive. May I touch it?'

I laughed, because that's some pretty funny stuff, then broke the bad news to Anna that I was 99 per cent certain that Philippe had long since removed his famous item of facial forestry. She waved aside my concerns, and told me I was talking rubbish. No man capable of growing a moustache as good as that would

. . . .

21 ...is a sentence you will not find opening a chapter of many other football books. I'm pretty happy with it.

ever remove it, she said. We should work on the assumption that he still had it. She asked me what I thought – not of her plan, which she insisted was watertight and my only viable option if I was serious about meeting Philippe Albert – but about her suggestion for my opening line to him. I told her I had my doubts; in particular, about whether I should really be asking to touch Philippe's (probably non-existent) moustache within seconds of meeting him. Anna nodded. She agreed it needed some work.

After 20 seconds or so of silent thought – although, what other sort of thought is there – she picked up her pen once more and began crossing through lines with relish. When she held the pad in front of my face, option four looked like this.

4. Just show up at Philippe's house with your sticker album. Learn the French for ~~'I'm sorry for this gross invasion of your privacy, Monsieur Albert. It was my girlfriend's idea.'~~
    ~~Also learn the French for~~ 'Your moustache is very impressive. May I touch it?'

'That's it,' she said. 'The plan and your opening line, finished.'

'It's not perfect.'

'Yes it is.'

'Why do I even need to say *anything* in French?' I asked. 'I know Philippe Albert speaks English.'

'He'll appreciate you making the effort.'

'Maybe.'

Anna frowned.

'And like I said: I'm 98 per cent sure he doesn't even have one anymore,' I added.

Anna's frown deepened.

'I just don't think I should open by asking to *touch* his moustache.'

Anna nodded, then picked up the pen and pad. I watched as she theatrically crossed out the word 'touching' and wrote 'brushing' instead. Touching was too intimate. Brushing was more practical, she said. And funnier.

Anna shut the notepad and declared the matter closed. I would travel to Belgium, doorstep Philippe Albert, and ask – in French – to brush his moustache. Whether he had one or not.

I left Anna's flat at around midnight. When I got home 15 minutes later, I booked a berth on the 27 April car ferry to France. I printed out my route from Dunkerque to the wee Belgian village of Wanfercée-Baulet. I copy-and-pasted the phrase 'Your moustache is very impressive. May I brush it?' into Google translate and familiarised myself with my lines:

'Votre moustache est très impressionnant. Puis-je brosser?'
'Votre moustache est très impressionnant. Puis-je brosser?'
'Votre moustache …'

You get the idea.

It was exciting, but for the first few cold seconds in bed, I stared out into the darkness and wondered why I had just done *any* of that. Part of me worried it was a foolish and reckless and unnecessary thing to do.

But I soon realised that when you've just decided to travel hundreds of miles to meet a retired Belgian centre-back who once chipped Peter Schmeichel, you don't need to ask *why*, because the *why* is obvious. I was about to travel hundreds of miles to meet a retired Belgian centre-back who once chipped Peter Schmeichel because travelling hundreds of miles to meet a retired Belgian centre-back who once chipped Peter Schmeichel was an *awesome* thing to do.

At least in theory, anyway. Soon I would find out for sure.

* * * * *

20 April 2012
Friday

I drove slowly down a pot-holey country road, flanked on both sides by green fields and greener trees. A bright midday sun danced across the shiny cover of *Premier League 96*, which was sat on the passenger seat beside me. Up ahead, the road looked like it was narrowing. I slowed down and listened as rough and ancient tarmac growled beneath my wheels. Actually, the car's wheels. I drove a little further. The edge of overgrown hedges clattered into my wing mirrors. Actually, the car's wing mirrors. I realised the road hadn't so much 'narrowed' as 'ended'. I reversed out of the bush before anyone besides me noticed my error.

I was lost. A few miles back, I had passed a mud-flecked sign that was at least written in the correct language. I had been driving in roughly the right direction for approximately the right number of hours, so I had to be close. As close as your face is to this book.

Or maybe further away, I wasn't sure exactly, because I had no way of checking my location. My sat-nav had no reception. Neither did my phone. All I knew for certain was that I was in the correct country.

But even that was difficult to confirm. I had already stopped and asked one local for some navigational guidance, but there was a language barrier – by which I mean that, while I spoke one, he didn't.

He communicated in grunts and fidgets alone, and was more interested in finding a place for his dog to relieve himself than he was in helping me.

'Excuse me,' I said, attempting to get the man's attention.

'Ughhrrrrhmmm,' he (sort of) replied, while dragging his odd and unusually small dog away to another patch of yellowing grass. I followed the pair of them, crawling along the kerb (in a non-soliciting, [*name redacted*]-esque way).

'I'm lost,' I said.

His dog stopped and circled his latest potential toilet, nose-down.

'Do you live here?'

The man said nothing.

'I need to find this address …' I held out a small piece of paper. The man took it, looked at it for less than a second, then shrugged and handed it back.

'Am I close?' I asked.

The man pretended not to have heard me.

'Do you speak English?'

The old man continued to shuffle forward, silently. He stopped, and patted the head of his little dog.

And then the little chap squatted down and quietly dropped his whiffy payload on to the grass.

Then the dog had a go too.

I left the pair of them alone after that. As I drove off, I watched them in my rear-view mirror. Well, their reflections if you're going to be a pedant about it. Neither of them cleared up after themselves, which was pretty rude, I thought.

I drove on and eventually found a little pub on a nominal main road, and inside, I found someone whom I could understand, and who could understand me. He told me I was 'two streets' away. So I drove two streets further. Then I realised I must have gone two streets in the wrong direction. I drove four roads back the way I had came until I finally found the street I had been searching for.

I parked my car. I found the right house. I rehearsed my risky opening line, and then I rehearsed my altogether safer back-up line. Finally, after a few deep and cleansing breaths (and a few shallow and dirtying thoughts that were in no way related to what I was about to do), I slipped *Premier League 96* into my bag and made for the front door of the house.

I knocked gently on the door, realised that knocking gently was pointless, then knocked loudly. For a few seconds, I waited in sticky-palmed silence. I knocked again. I fidgeted through a few more seconds of palpitating hush.

As I raised my fist to complete my hat-trick of knocks, the door swung open. A man, one whom I recognised instantly, was standing before me. On his face was a warm, welcoming smile. Also on his face were a pair of eyes, a nose, some ears tucked away around the side, and a whole host of the usual facial miscellany you normally get (e.g. eyebrows, etc) on a face.

But what I really noticed was what was missing. There was *no* moustache. There was literally not a moustache on his face. Imagine the biggest moustache in the world. Now imagine it not being there. That's what it was like. There wasn't even a wispy myth of a 'tache like the one Gary Neville occasionally wears. Nothing. I will be so annoyed if I've not made that clear.

I went with my non-risky opening line, and just said 'Hi, I'm Adam,' before extending my hand. Not in an Inspector Gadget way, but a regular, hand-shakey way. He shook it.

And then I realised something important.

This wasn't Philippe Albert's house.

And this wasn't Philippe Albert.

This wasn't even Belgium.

This was Gloucestershire.

And this was Gary Penrice's house.

The man in front of me was 'Porno' himself.
In the flesh.
Not literally.
He doesn't take the nickname that seriously.

* * * * *

Before we go any further, I want to apologise for misleading you temporarily there. It is an old literary technique, also used in the equally lame worlds of magic and politics, called misdirection or 'lying'. That old man didn't take a crap on the ground beside his also-dumping dog, either. But he did ignore me in my hour of navigational need, so I feel no guilt about making you think he did.

My trip to Belgium was still a week away, and in the time between booking that trip and right now, Gary Penrice had fallen into my lap with the minimum of fuss (i.e. none).

But that's how it goes with non-fiction. Sometimes the story just happens, unspectacularly. I can't just throw in a war or some foxy boxing if I want to up the narrative and dramatic ante. I am sorry about that. But stick with me. There will be some jelly wrestling and boat chases later on though. And more Groucho Marx-inspired dangling modifiers like that one, too. I have no idea what a jelly boat chase is.

Anyway, a few weeks previous – while I had been e-mailing and tweeting anybody with even the most cursory relationship to one of my missing five – I had stumbled across an interview with Gary Penrice on a site called watfordlegends.com. I had e-mailed the site's owner, Dan, asking if he was still in touch with TAFKAP[22]. I explained what I was up to, and asked if Dan might be able to put me in touch with Gary.

---

22 *The Artist Formerly Known As Porno*. Said aloud, that anagram sounds like Welsh headgear: like a top hat with a leek attached, or a Stetson with a really good singing voice.

FROM: Dan, Watfordlegends.com
TO: Me
Hi Adam,

Yes, we are still in contact with Gary. I will drop him a line later on and see if he minds me passing his number on to you. He is a great character to talk to!

Once I have heard back from him I will be in touch with you.
Cheers,
Dan.

Great news, I thought to myself. I decided to tell Dan, too.

FROM: Me
TO: Dan, Watfordlegends.com
Thanks Dan. Great news!
Cheers!
Adam

An hour or two later, this reply pinged into my inbox.

FROM: Dan, Watfordlegends.com
TO: Me
All sorted. His number is 07xxxxxxxx.

As easy as that, I had Gary Penrice's telephone number. If I had known it was this easy to find footballers back in the mid-1990s, I would have saved my pocket money and just met every footballer in my Merlin albums in person.

I dialled the number and Gary answered. After I got over the surprise of a phone number containing that many 'Xs' actually working, I told him about my sticker book quest. He told me he would love to help me out, and that I could make the trip up (and across, if you want to be precise) to his place in deepest Gloucestershire as soon as I wanted. He would be happy to pose up for a picture and help me get a little closer to finally completing my sticker album.

I thought back to his Wikipedia entry. No wonder he was so well-respected in the village community. He was indeed a friendly and helpful man.

SIX

* * * * *

Gary and I settled down in his lounge with cups of tea – Gary on a comfy-looking leather recliner in the corner of the room, me on a sofa to his left. Outside, the usual stuff was going on: the sun was shining, a breeze was blowing. Some natural things – trees, bushes, some different trees to the first lot – were also knocking about.

Just as I had with Stuart, I started the conversation by asking Gary about his career. He had started as an apprentice with his local club, Bristol City, but after failing to make the grade at Ashton Gate, he had dropped down into non-league football. After a successful spell with Mangotsfield United – a team with a name straight from *Roy of the Rovers* – he was snapped up by his home town's other club, signing his first pro deal with Bristol Rovers in 1984.

Five successful years later, he joined top-flight Watford for a cool half-a-million pounds before moving to Aston Villa for an even cooler one million bucks two years later. Just eight months after moving to the Midlands, he was on the move again, this time to Queens Park Rangers, the page from which his smiling and moustachioed face was missing in my *Premier League 96* album.

I showed Gary the space in my sticker album where his sticker should have been. He laughed and told me that in early November – roughly around the time when Merlin would have had to finalise the line-up of each team in the album – Gary was sold to Watford. He had barely kicked a ball for QPR that season. He shouldn't have even been in the album in the first place.

This, I grumbled aloud, was annoying. I was frustrated and angry. But then I remembered that tsunamis and tornadoes and mimes still existed in this ridiculous world, and I calmed down. Gary Penrice's erroneous inclusion in and subsequent absence from my sticker album wasn't really comparable to any of those horrible things. And besides, he wasn't going to be absent for much longer.

But before the picture, there was some talking to be done. Mainly by Gary, but that was fine by me: he was a fascinating, funny, friendly and (f)interesting man. My sticker album had apparently got him thinking about his career. He had some stories to tell me.

'When I started my career at Bristol Rovers,' he said, 'the club was so skint we had lads playing for us who worked during the week in the Rolls-Royce and British Airways factories, or on the railways. Everyone had a trade back then, as well as their football, because there was no money in the game.

'I was doing my plumbing courses because I wasn't even sure I'd have a career in the game. At Rovers, we had an electrician up front, me with my plumbing, another lad who worked in a laundry place – we could have built and run a house with that team. I wouldn't have wanted to live in it, but we could have done. We had every sort of tradesman in there.

'In fact, I remember we had one lad who played a game for us in the late 80s – I forget his name – but he scored against Chesterfield on his debut. The next game was Wigan away, and he got taken off at half-time. He was pretty wound up about it and he just comes out and says to the manager, "I don't need this hassle, I'm an electrician. I'm off." He left after that and we never saw him again. He could make more money as an electrician, so he went back to that – and this was in what is now called League 1. That's what it was like back then.'

'More innocent, I suppose. And less serious, maybe?' I said.

'They were strange times; more innocent times, definitely. Twenty-five years ago, football used to have a nice innocence to it. That's gone now. Don't get me wrong – it's a good thing the game has moved on from that, because if things had stayed like that, football would be in a right state now.

'But in those days, there was more room for footballers to be characters – to be themselves, really – because the game was more connected to the real world. We were closer to the fans, so we could interact with them more easily. They related to us, too, I think, because we weren't that different to them. But that's not the case anymore. My ambition was to play to 35 and save some money. Footballers are celebrities now, aren't they? I don't envy them at all.'

'Not even with all the money they earn?' I asked.

'They earn amazing money, that's true, but to be honest, I didn't become a footballer because I wanted to be rich. I just wanted to play football. The money is nice, but it's temporary. The important things I got from football are my memories –

of scoring goals; promotions; even losing games. *That* is what football is about to me. When I meet up with old team-mates, no-one says, "Hey, remember when I signed that big contract and then bought that car?"

'We talk about the games, good and bad, big and small. And to be honest, I felt disengaged from my friends once I started earning more than them. Some of my mates were unemployed or not earning very much, and that was difficult to handle.

'When I started earning decent money, I bought a nice house in a nice estate but I felt out of place. The fella next to me was a scientist who had worked hard for 50-odd years doing important, difficult stuff and I was a 25-year-old bloke who kicked a football for a living. I was just a footballer, but it was like being a lottery winner. I felt removed from where I felt I should have been. Do you know what I mean?'

I thought of Gary's empty space in my album, and nodded. I knew exactly what he was talking about.

Art, 2

PROFESSIONAL
FOWL.

Seven

GARY AND I finished our cups of tea and moved into his back garden. Temporarily moved. We weren't setting up camp or building a bungalow or anything. He squinted into the low spring sun and I snapped away with my camera. As I inspected the picture, I told him I might have to draw a moustache on the printed version later on. He laughed and said that was fine. He wished me luck with the rest of my sticker book, and told me to take a biscuit for the journey home.

GARY PENRICE

'So anyway,' he said, as we made our way back through the house and out on to Gary's driveway where my cat was parked. 'Why are you doing this sticker album thing?'

'Er, well …' I spluttered, 'I'm not sure, really.'

'You're not sure?'

'Well, the album is incomplete, so it seems the obvious thing to do is to complete it. That's all I've got so far.'

Gary smiled a smile that seemed to suggest that, even if I didn't quite know why I was doing this, he did.

(Did I just write 'where my cat was parked'?)

'It's a bit of an adventure, isn't it?' he said.

'So far, yes,' I replied. 'I've just been sitting in your front room eating biscuits, and a few weeks ago Stuart Ripley bought me a brownie.'

(I did, cat!)

'That's something that's gone from the game too – the romance, the adventure. Like, you see teams nowadays – not just the big teams, but smaller teams too – putting out reserve teams in the cups. And I sometimes hear fans and players saying things like "our priority is to stay in the Prem", or that they'd rather just avoid relegation from the Premier League every year than actually win a cup. They say "a cup run is a distraction", don't they? That's not right.

'And it's all about "winning ugly" nowadays, isn't it? Most of the teams in the Premier League play defensive football and try to nick a goal from a set-piece. I understand that: they have to do what's best for their clubs, but it's not always great to watch, is it?

'Don't get me wrong: the Premier League is a great product. We've got some of the best stadiums, the best players and some of the biggest clubs in the world, but for a lot of the teams in the Premier League, it's just about getting to 40 points, isn't it?

'As a player, you wanted to go on cup runs and fans wanted to go to Wembley. Because at the end of the day, that's what football is about isn't it? It's about more than just winning and losing, it's about dreaming. D'you know what I mean?'

'I do,' I said.

(I meant 'car', obviously. I didn't park my 'cat' anywhere.)

'Out of interest – who are the other players you need to find?' Gary asked.

I reeled off the now familiar but quickly-shortening list, 'Scott Minto, Philippe Albert, Lars Bohinen, and Keith Curle.'

'Keith Curle?'

'Keith Curle.'

'Keith Curle!'

'Keith Curle.'

'Me and Keith were best mates at school!'

I made this face (turn the book – or your own face – 90 degrees to the left)

:o

'I've known him since I was a kid. We played football together as nippers.'

I continued to make this face (and turn again)

:o

'Next time I speak to him, I'll get him to give you a call.'

And then I made this face (and once more, thanks)

:D

I thought back, for the second time that afternoon, to Gary's Wikipedia entry. No wonder he was considered such a 'friendly and respected member' of his community. He had been incredibly accommodating and now, I respected him a great deal too.

And as far as I was concerned, he more than lived up to his 'Porno' nickname, too. I drove home to Southsea that afternoon a very happy and satisfied man.

Because of the sticker, not because of any 'porno' related reason. Nothing like that. At all. I hope I'm making that clear.

(*I don't even own a cat.*)

* * * * *

21 April 2012
Saturday

'Duh-duh-duh-duhhh, duhduh-duh-duh-duhhh, duh-duhhh, duh-duhhh-duh-duh …'

'Nope,' said Anna.

'Duh-duh-duh-duhhh, duhduh-duh-duh-duhhh, duh-duhhh, duh-duhhh-duh-duh …'

'Still no.'

'Duh-duh-duh-duhhh, duhduh-duh-duh-duhhh, duh-duhhh, duh-duhhh-duh-duh …'

'No.'

'Come on!' I said. 'That's how it goes. It's *so* famous.'

'Sorry. I've never seen it.'

'Unbelievable.'

'And it's *just* football?'

'And some talking.'

'Some talking?'

'Yeah. About tactics and that sort of thing. *Analysis.*'

'And it lasts for how long?'

'About an hour and a quarter.'

'Every week?!'

'Every week of the season, yes. Anyway, it's starting.'

The actual *Match of the Day* theme tune began to play. I looked at Anna and waited for her to tell me how accurate my earlier performance had been. She said nothing, which I took as an insult. The opening credits continued to roll.

'Who's that?' she asked.

'Bob Wilson.'

'And him?'

'Kevin Keegan.'

'Philippe Albert's old manager?'

'That's him, yes.'

'And the bloke doing back-flips?'

'Kenwyne Jones.'

'Ken …?'

'Ken*wyne.*'

'Sounds Welsh.'

'He's not.'

The theme tune ended and the camera panned around the *MOTD* studios. Gary Lineker began to speak. He talked about that day's games being crucial in 'the race for fourth' and the 'race for fourth from bottom'. Lineker introduced Alans Hansen and Shearer. I looked at Anna. She was frowning. I remembered I still had the biscuit Gary Penrice had given me for the journey. I gave it to Anna as a present.

'Is Alan a popular footballer name?'

I thought about it for a second. Thompson, Wright, Judge, Ball, Knight, Smith (x2). I told her it sort of was, but less so than this programme might suggest. Of the three ex-footballers in the studio, 66 per cent were called Alan. That kind of percentage was unrepresentative, I said.

The highlights of the opening game, Newcastle versus Stoke, played out. After the goals had been scored – two for Yohan Cabaye and one for Papiss Cisse, assisted by Cabaye with a brilliant through ball – I asked Anna what she thought so far. She said she was enjoying it. She said that football – or football highlights at least – seemed exciting and loud and fun, like Formula 1, only exciting and fun too. After the post-match interviews with players and managers, the cameras cut back to the studio.

'What's happening now?' she asked.

'This is the talking bit,' I said.

'The analysis?'

'Yes.'

Anna watched silently for a few moments.

'This is boring.'

'I know.'

'Which Alan is this?'

'Shearer.'

'He's *very* boring. He looks like a policeman.'

'Yeah.'

'He's just describing exactly what's happening on the screen but doing it in a more boring voice than the commentator.'

'Basically.'

'Is that football analysis?'

'That's what it's closest to.'

The analysis mercifully ended, and the next game – Tottenham versus QPR at Loftus Road – began. Once again, Anna watched and fired intermittent questions at me.

'Do footballers get a discount on sleeve tattoos?'

'They're very popular with footballers. So maybe.'

'That one there,' she said, pointing at the screen. 'He is one of the few who doesn't have a sleeve tattoo. Who is he?'

'Which one?'

'The one there. He looks like a small witch.'

'That's Luka Modric.'

'Luka Mod-Witch.'

'Nice.'

'And who is that?' she said, pointing again.

'Bobby Zamora.'

'He looks like the eagle in *The Muppets*.'

The highlights ended. QPR had held on for a 1-0 win and afterwards, Harry Redknapp had a little moan and Mark Hughes did a brilliant impression of a very boring man. Then we cut back to the studio, and this time, straight into Alan Hansen on analysis duties. He was talking about the wind or some passes or a header or something.

'This bit is *so* boring,' said Anna, with unerring accuracy.

'Yeah. It absolutely is.'

'Why don't they just show the goals?'

I shrugged: 'I don't know.'

'They don't even need a presenter. They could just flash up a graphic – "Norwich vs. Blackburn Rangers" – or whatever …'

'Rovers.'

'How could *that* matter?'

'It does. But I agree.'

'I mean look at Gary Lineker,' said Anna. 'He has the same face as those trolls you used to put on the end of pencils. The ones with the luminous hair, only his hair is grey. And I don't need a man with the face of a children's toy to introduce the goals. Do you?'

'Nope.'

'And these two complete Alans are even worse. It's like someone has cast a spell that's brought two Marks & Spencers men's department mannequins to life.'

'Maybe Luka Mod-Witch did it.'

'Well played.'

'Thanks.'

'And the name of the show is wrong,' she continued. 'It should be *Goals of the Day*, because I just want to see the goals – and, actually, any fights or footage of people getting a ball to the face from close range. But mainly goals. They should call it *Goals and Fights of the Day*.'

I was very proud. She sounded like a true football fan already.

We sat through a few more highlights – Blackburn v Norwich, Bolton v Swansea, Fulham v Harchester, and Hufflepuff v Ravenclaw – before Anna lost interest and fell asleep.

I stayed up to watch *The Football League Show* while Anna, now in a foetal little ball on the sofa, snoozed away.

I didn't want to stay up, but I had to, out of loyalty. Today had been a bad day – a day when something unpleasant had taken place. Watching the highlights was a part of the healing process.

Pompey had lost 2-1 at home to Derby County, and the defeat sealed what had long been on the cards. For the first time since before I was born – and just four years after winning the FA Cup with a team of highly-paid international stars (and Noe Pamarot) – Portsmouth Football Club had been demoted to the third tier of the English football pyramid. Worse outcomes loomed, too. The club was facing liquidation. There was no money. We were football's Bluth Company.

I hadn't been to Fratton Park much during the season. My love for the club remained undiminished, but a combination of work and finances and laziness had prevented me from watching Pompey live all that often. In previous years, my position as a freelance football reporter ensured my attendance card remained regularly stamped. But now that I was working in the advertising world, that particular avenue had, if not closed entirely, then narrowed.

But my absence from the ground didn't ease the pain of relegation. It was rubbish. The Premier League years had ended in a mess of debt and excess, but in the two years since, things had – impossibly – deteriorated even further.

It was a surprise to see the Pompey club badge still read just 'Portsmouth FC' – the club could have changed its name to 'Crisis Club Portsmouth FC' or 'Cash-strapped Portsmouth FC' and no-one would have noticed. It had been a very long time since anyone had mentioned the club in conversation without adding one of those prefixes.

As I watched the highlights and listened to the commentary confirming the news of relegation, I felt nothing. The club was such a shambles off the pitch, that results had ceased to mean anything on it. I felt guilty for thinking it, but I almost welcomed the relegation. The club needed to bottom out, and then to start again. I still wanted Pompey to be successful, but success seemed impossible right now. We needed a complete overhaul and it felt as though that might only happen when the club had hit rock-bottom.

I eased myself upright on the sofa, careful not to wake Anna, and pulled *Premier League 96* from my bag. As I flicked through the pages, I thought about how much more innocent and straightforward the game had been back then. I began to wonder, again, why I was so fixed on completing my sticker album.

But as I did, Anna woke up suddenly. She noticed *Premier League 96*, open on my lap. Then she noticed the confused grimace on my face. She told me I looked as though I was trying to find a greater significance in my sticker album quest than was necessary. I told her she was very perceptive to have noticed that.

She sat up and leaned over for a closer look at the album. She picked the book up and flicked through it for a few minutes. Suddenly, she stopped on the Sheffield Wednesday page. She stared at it intensely, then asked me who John Sheridan was. I asked her why she was asking, and she just shrugged. She flicked through a few more pages, eventually stopping on the Arsenal page.

'Him, here,' she said, pointing to a sticker on the left-hand page.

'Martin Keown?'

'Yeah, him,' she said, looking at him with her head cocked to one side.

'What about him?' I asked.

'He looks like someone drew a frowny face on the side of a cliff.'

Pretty funny and pretty accurate. Anna handed me back the album and rolled back over on to her side. She snuggled back into the foetal position, and fell asleep.

Jokes, 16–18.

Which footballer is famous for his charity work with animals? Dan Petrescue.

Torquay United were known as Silent Picture United until 1927.[23]

Keith Fahey's a jolly good fellow. Which nobody can deny.

. . . .
23 One for all the Al Jolson fans.

Eight

'When are you off?'

'Tomorrow afternoon.'

'And the plan …?'

'… is to show up at his house on Saturday.'

'With the sticker album … ?'

'Yes.'

'And a French phrase … ?'

'Votre moustache est très impressionnant. Puis-je brosser?'

'And then you're going to ask him to pose for a picture … ?'

'That's right.'

'OK.'

'Does Anna know you're doing this?'

'Of course. It was her idea. Because she is wonderful and beautiful and …'

'OK, OK.'

'Sorry.'

'Does Rosh know you're doing this?'

'No, he does not. He thinks I'm working from home tomorrow.'

'Right. So if he asks … ?'

'Don't tell him I'm in Brussels.'

'*Don't* tell him?'

'Don't. What he doesn't know, won't hurt him.'

'Hmm. I think that's specious reasoning.'

'Thank you.'

'Well, good luck.'

I laughed. 'Luck is for the ill-prepared, Ed.'

'Is it?'

'Yeah. It's a saying.'

'Oh right. Well, good luck.'

'Thanks.'

'Hey Adam, did you know Henry VIII liked horse riding, jousting and archery?' asked Ed.

'I did not,' I replied.

* * * * *

27 April 2012
Friday

My room inside the dirt-cheap B&B was *very* small. My television had seven channels of snowy static and not much else on it. The lightbulb in my bedside lamp was broken. Through the gently rattling window to the left of my bed, the sweet aroma of *frites mayonnaise*, expensive chocolate, waffles and Herman Van Rompuy wafted in. This was definitely Belgium.

Philippe Albert was still not picking up his phone, but I wasn't concerned. Not yet anyway, because I was feeling too good about this trip to let any negative thoughts in. Sure, the ferry crossing had been a bit odd, but I had come through it in roughly the same state in which I started it (enthusiastic), which is more than could be said for Brian McClair. He was covered in bird crap. If you skipped the prologue, this won't mean a thing to you. But that's on you. You should have read it.

Philippe Albert's home address was safely stored in my sat-nav, and the next morning, I would venture out into the Belgium countryside to find him. As a back-up I had the stadium addresses for all three of his former clubs in Belgium: Charleroi, Anderlecht and KV Mechelen, which sounded less like a football club and more like a Scandinavian crime-noir writer. If he wasn't at home, someone at one of those grounds might know where he was. Maybe. Probably not, but maybe.

I had managed to get through the working day unscathed. I told Rosh my mobile was broken, so the only way to reach me was by e-mail. I had managed to make a cup of coffee in a Brussels cafe last long enough to get my work done and Rosh seemed happy enough. As far as he knew, I was sat at home in Southsea. I felt bad for pulling the wool over his eyes, but telling him where I *really* was would only have complicated matters. Also, I *didn't* actually feel bad for pulling the wool over his eyes, which made doing it that much easier.

It was Friday night and I was in the capital of Belgium, alone, with literally dozens of Euros in my bum bag. I didn't really feel like staying in – I realised the lightbulb in my bedside lamp was less broken, more not there – so I walked to a nearby bar to escape the gloom of my room.

As I walked into the bar, I suddenly felt as though I was doing something very wrong. What was the legal drinking age in Belgium? Was it 30? I thought it might be 30. I worried I might not get served. Perhaps Philippe had grown his moustache to get around Belgium's crazy-high legal drinking age.

I sat down on a small table near the door, and when a waiter came over, I asked for a beer, in French. He came back a minute later with a beer. Success. I pulled a crisp ten euro note from my bum bag and paid. I checked the legal drinking age later. It wasn't 30.

For an hour or so, I nursed my drink in the incredibly quiet bar and day-dreamed about how tomorrow might go. I tried to imagine how I might feel when I knocked on the door and finally saw Philippe Albert, the man himself, stood before me. I practised my opening line under my breath.

'Votre moustache est très impressionnant. Puis-je brosser?'

It was sounding good.

'Votre moustache est très impressionnant. Puis-je brosser?'

I was getting confident with it. My accent was getting stronger. I chuckled to myself. Anna was right, Philippe probably *would* appreciate such an unusual welcome.

'Votre moustache est très impressionnant. Puis-je brosser?' I said.

I was suddenly aware that the table beside me had stopped talking. The people sitting at the table. The table was just standing there. It hadn't said a word so far, and probably wouldn't any time soon, either.

The three people sitting at the table, however, were staring at me, grinning. This, I realised, was pretty embarrassing. I had been busted by some Belgians whispering to myself about wanting to brush someone's 'impressive moustache'.

I did the only thing fitting in the circumstances. I finished my beer with a gulp, stood up and bowed deeply, holding my pose for a few seconds as though this had been a very important piece of outsider art. Then I did it again. And again.

They didn't applaud, which was a shame. If this had been France they would have done, I thought to myself. If only my French friend from the ferry had been here with his camera. He would have been able to add 'garçon demande à brosser la moustache de l'homme invisible' to his earlier masterwork 'garçon sur un ferry, avec un livre couvert de merde d'oiseaux'.

One of them asked, in English, why I was repeating the same phrase over and over. I thought about lying – 'I am a blimp salesman who is hoping to impress a big potential client tomorrow. He has a very big moustache which he likes to have brushed by potential business partners. I am practising my French …' – but in the end, I decided that was too complicated. They looked like a nice bunch (apart from one of them who looked like he might start juggling at any moment and expect people to be impressed) so I decided to be honest with them.

'I can tell you the real reason,' I said. 'But it's a long story. Actually, it's not that long at the moment; this will probably only be about chapter eight,' I added, presciently.

A few minutes later, they were up to speed. As I finished explaining why I was in Belgium, muttering under my breath about moustaches, they laughed, loudly.

'That is funny,' said one of them, helpfully explaining the loud laughter.

. 'Very *English*,' said another. By which I assumed he meant 'eccentric' rather than 'closed-minded and sexually repressed'.

The third one, also a Brit, said nothing. I noticed he was circulating two small and brightly coloured balls in his right hand. I also noticed that, while he thought no-one was looking, he picked his nose and ate it.

'Do you like juggling?' he asked. I told him I didn't.

For the next few hours, I drank Belgian lager and talked Belgian football with my new friends Jay, a Brit, and Marc, a Belgian. The juggling man, whose name I didn't get nor particularly want but was almost certainly Alan, left momentarily, apparently in search of someone who wanted to watch him throw and catch small balls to no discernible conclusion. That is jugglers for you, total dicks, each and every one. Unless *you* happen to be one, in which case I'm sure you're the exception that proves the rule. Probably not though.

After a lively discussion about Belgium's World Cup chances ('good') and England's ('less good'), talk turned to the Premier League, the title race and then, obviously enough, to football stickers.

I asked Jay and Marc if they had ever collected them when they were children. They nodded, to indicate that they *had* collected football stickers when they were children. I asked if either of them had ever completed an album. Both shook their head from side to side to indicate that they had *not* completed an album. At that moment, their juggling friend returned, and I used that opportunity to use the bathroom. When I returned, Jay and Marc had bought another round of beers.

'Who else do you need to find, after you've met Philippe Albert?' asked Marc.

I reeled off the list. They didn't react to any of the names with anything other than polite nods. Alan the juggler butted into the conversation.

'Can't you just buy the stickers?' he asked.

'No. The album is 16 years old. They don't make the stickers anymore. And buying them would be cheating, anyway.'

'Cheating?'

'Yes. Cheating.'

'OK … Can you get a photo of the player from the internet and stick it in?' he asked.

'That is cheating too,' said Jay. I liked Jay.

'And not fun,' said Marc. I liked Marc, too.

'It's supposed to be a challenge. If it was too easy, it wouldn't be a challenge. It would be a joke, a folly, a waste of time. The Scottish Premier League, basically,' I said, repetitiously.

The Juggler – who sounds like the worst Batman villain ever – looked at me blankly.

'Or juggling,' I added, under my breath.

* * * * *

EIGHT

Wanfercée-Baulet was a nondescript place. Rows of scruffy houses, some boarded up, probably abandoned, sat within spitting distance/a stone's throw of grander homes backing on to rich green countryside. I know that because I tried. My spit and some stones made the journey very successfully. I annoyed a few Belgians, but I was an Englishman abroad. They expected it from me.

The village seemed to be little more than a mile square, and its petiteness (Microsoft Word says that isn't a legitimate word, but language is a constantly evolving thing, so up yours, Bill Gates) filled me with confidence that I had definitely found *the* Philippe Albert.

There was more chance of me taking up juggling than there being two people with the same name living here. No matter where I drove in the village, I was probably less than 800 yards from where I should have been. I could have stopped my car, shouted Philippe Albert's name and followed his shouted reply until I found him.

And yet somehow, I was lost. As I always seem to be. I don't think I've ever aimed for a place and arrived there without going to another, entirely wrong place first, second, third and sometimes fourth. How I won the sperm race, I have no idea.

My sat-nav had taken me to a beautiful church, complete with tall spire cutting into the watery blue sky, which was sat on the edge of a little square. There were some houses opposite, but this was not the right road. This was not where I had to be.

'Philippe Albert!' I shouted.

Maybe it would work.

It didn't.

So I drove on. I got a bit road-ragey (also not a word, apparently) at a Belgian for driving on the wrong (right) side of the road, realised *I* was on the wrong (left) side of the road, corrected my mistake and hoped nobody had noticed.

Somebody had, however. A middle-aged man in smart clothes shouted at me from the side of the road. In his hand was a stone, in his other hand a piece of shattered glass. He seemed to be accusing me of spitting on his house. I drove away quickly.

And as I did, I spotted the road I had been looking for. I turned into it, scanned the doors and post boxes for house numbers, and finally found the one I had been looking for, which was pretty lucky as this chapter was beginning to drag a little.

I parked up and for a second or two, thought about what I had done (driven from my house in Southsea to a small village in rural(ish) Belgium) and what I was about to do (knock on the door of a house in a small village in rural(ish) Belgium, take a photo of the man who lived there, then drive back to my house in Southsea).

But instead of a wave of excitement, I felt a great shake of sudden anxiety sweep over me – the sort I normally only ever feel at the onset of a panic attack, or whenever I hear Tim Lovejoy's voice. Something was wrong.

* * * * *

In April 2010, Pompey beat Spurs 2-0 at Wembley to reach a second FA Cup Final in three years. I was there, sat on my own among strangers, just as I was now in Wanfercée-Baulet. The game was a tense, scrappy affair, made all the more nerve-jangling because of the company I was keeping. To my right was a young family, with their two children. They were nice enough. But to my left was a man, maybe 40 years of age, also on his own. He was less nice.

It was a 4pm kick-off, but he appeared to have been drinking non-stop for at least six or seven years before the game. His shirt was torn slightly at the shoulder and wrapped around his right forearm was a grubby, slowly-unravelling bandage. He used the c-word with such ferocious regularity it made the parents to my right visibly wince.

I began to wonder if he was a non-native English speaker who had learned the language by watching Malcolm Tucker on *The Thick of It*. He was utterly terrifying and so packed full of testosterone that simply being near him put a hair on my chest. Which made three. Under normal circumstances, I would have crossed the road to avoid him.

But when Pompey took the lead in extra time through a Frédéric Piquionne goal, something strange happened. As a juddering roar rattled Wembley's windows, I leapt into a bear-hug with this bruised and boozed man. Before I knew it, he had me in a happy headlock. A millisecond later, he had smacked a great slobbery kiss on the top of my head. And all the while, I punched the air with joy and screamed myself hoarse. I was so caught up in the moment, I really didn't mind. Not even as I felt the rough scrape of his bandage against the side of my face.

But as the primal wave of winning noise receded and his grip on the sides of my head loosened, I suddenly returned to my senses. I was aware once more of where I was, and of what had just happened; I was stood next to a very frightening man who had just clamped me in a celebratory headlock and kissed me on the top of my head. The moment of madness had passed. All that remained was a slightly awkward feeling of embarrassment.

And so it was now. On the car ferry over, and as I drove through France and into Belgium, as I drank with Marc and Jay and as I set off in the early morning mist to Wanfercée-Baulet, I had been filled with relentless enthusiasm. This, I was convinced, was going to be an away trip to remember; a European adventure that was glamorous and spontaneous and ultimately, would prove to be a success, too.

But as I stood on a quiet street in a tiny Belgian village, I was suddenly aware of where I was. I was aware of what I was about to do. And it struck me as a bit weird.

For a split-second – about *that* long – I thought about getting in my car and turning right back around. But before I could slap down those feelings of uncertainty, I realised I was already walking towards Philippe Albert's front door. I was walking towards it, and I was raising my hand and forming it into a fist, ready to knock on it.

I knocked, and waited.

I pulled my jacket straight and practiced my opening line. Saying it out loud, even quietly to myself, made me lose my nerve. I abandoned the plan immediately. I would speak to him, in English, and say something normal. Maybe 'hello' or 'hi' or 'sorry to bother you, Mr Albert'. Whatever. The one thing I would not ask Philippe Albert would be if I could brush the moustache I *knew* he no longer had. I couldn't. Well, I could, but I wasn't going to.

Twenty seconds had passed.

I knocked again.

Behind the door – it was a nice door, wood, hinged, the tiniest bit smaller than the door frame, as most of the best doors are – I thought I could hear the rhythmic clomp of footsteps over creaky floorboards.

But another ten seconds passed.

Still nothing.

Now, if I was the sort of writer who tailored the weather conditions to match the mood of the scene, I would probably say that a sudden and chilly breeze swept up, and grey clouds began to mass overhead. Actually, it was pretty mild.

I stepped back from the door and looked for signs of life – an open window, a television left on, some humans living inside – but the house was absolutely quiet. I called the residential telephone number I had found in the *White Pages*. From the doorstep, I could hear it gently ringing, which meant two things. One, that this was definitely the right house. And two, that this house was definitely empty.

I thought back to that FA Cup semi-final. The same temporary fog of insanity that had descended on me then, and had been hovering over me from Southsea through France and on to a small street in Wanfercée-Baulet, had well and truly lifted. I had travelled hundreds of miles from home, for absolutely no reason. Like Stephen Warnock at the 2010 World Cup. No-one was home.

Jokes, 19–21.

Which footballer worked in puppetry before turning pro? Jason Puncheon-Judy.

Which footballer only eats bread, pasta and potatoes? Benito Carbonly.

Which ex-Liverpool defender is now a very lenient exam grader? Mark Wright.

Nine

OR THE next few hours, I waited. When the waiting got too boring and soul-destroying, I went for a walk and found a little convenience store. Inside, I bought some food, a Belgian lottery scratchcard and a hilariously dull postcard for Anna (just a picture of some stones). I popped the latter two in my bum bag and the first one in my mouth, and headed back to my car.

During the course of 180 or so increasingly quiet minutes, I taught myself how to whistle. That sounds like bull*[bleep]*, but I really did. After 20-some years of trying and failing, I finally succeeded. I whistled the theme from *Jurassic Park* to celebrate. Phwee-hoo-phwee-hoo-hoo, phwee-hoo-phwee-hoo-hoo. Just like that.

I also carried out a few experiments. I worked out that if I put enough coins (25) in my pockets and then jogged at a brisk enough pace (a bit faster than a quite old dog running), I could become a human tambourine. On a quiet and empty road not far from Philippe's house, I worked out how far back I could move the driver's seat and still maintain control of the vehicle. Actually, I worked out how far I could move my seat back and *not* maintain control of the vehicle, but by doing that, I worked out the first thing as well. I put the dashboard heaters in my car on full-blast and timed how long it took to make a regular cheese sandwich into a toasted one.

The result was still pending by the time the sun began to fall. Or set. Whatever. It was getting dark, is the point, and there remained no cars on the driveway, no lights on inside the house, and no people to be seen. I hope I'm making that clear.

My ferry back to England wasn't until the following evening, but this was still a decidedly *merde* (or *[bleep]* if you're reading the

French translation) state of affairs, and I was angry. Frustrated. No, angry. I did what I nearly always did in this sort of situation. I sent an e-mail.

> To: FIFA
> From: Me
> Hi FIFA, Adam again.
>
> This time I'm in Belgium. I came over here hoping to meet the former Newcastle centre-back Philippe Albert, but again, something has gone awry.
>
> Sure, it's probably partly my fault for just showing up on his doorstep without having first established some telephone contact, but I am still 100% certain that somehow this is your fault too, Count Blatter.
>
> Therefore, I have once again enclosed my travel expenses – car ferry ticket to France, petrol, hotel bill, and a receipt for some bread and (slow-to-melt) cheese.
>
> I will accept payment by cheque, BACS transfer or total control over the next re-branding of the Europa League.[24]
>
> Cheers,
>
> Adam
>
> P.S. Any news on the Cup Winners' Cup thing?

* * *

29 April 2012
Sunday

It was freezing. I was raining. Or the other way around. My car smelt of slowly-perspiring cheese and a (less) slowly-perspiring me. I was in a jam. A pickle. A third food-related idiom. Maybe a chutney. But a bad one. One made of guns and spiders.

Things were not going to plan. The plan, in case you need reminding, was that I would toddle over to Belgium, drive to Philippe Albert's house and knock on his door. He would answer it, wearing his Newcastle kit and his 1996 vintage moustache,

. . . .

24 'The Continental Challenge, in association with Little Chef' or 'The Little Chef Continental Challenge'. The new trophy will be a nine-hundred-foot-high silver croissant. Games will be decided by lottery/fist fights at UEFA headquarters.

which I would then offer to brush lovingly. He would accept my kind offer and we would become firm friends. We would talk football, he would pose for a photograph for my sticker album, and I would return to England triumphant, and halfway (or 3/6, if you prefer) towards finding my missing six (or 530 minus 524, if you prefer).

But none of that was happening. Sure, I had driven over to Belgique and made it as far as his door. I had knocked on it too. But if a man knocks on a door and no-one is there to hear it, has he really knocked on it? Well, yes. But he may as well not have.

Sunday was following much the same pattern as Saturday. I felt the same rush of excitement and embarrassment as I made the walk from my car to Philippe's front door. I knocked and waited. Then I knocked again. More waiting. More private philosophical debate about whether a man knocking on a door to an empty house is really knocking on it. The answer was still 'yes', but he still may as well not have been.

I trudged back to my car and slumped into my seat. I had learned my lesson about giving up and leaving too soon from my experience in Manchester with Stuart. But hope – and my own reserves of enthusiasm – was evaporating fast.

I called Anna.

'How's it going?' she asked. 'Better than yesterday?'

'About as good.'

'That bad?'

'Yes. I don't know what to do.'

'For now, you just have to stay patient.'

'But he's *definitely* not here.'

'He will be. Sit tight. Oh, some post arrived for you, at my flat.'

'At *your* flat? Addressed to *me*?'

'Yeah.'

'Weird. I'll open it when I get back. But what should I do now? Should I go to the stadiums instead?'

'You can e-mail them. Or call them. Stay there. That's his house. Probably. He'll show up.'

'He won't.'

'He will. Stay positive.'

I thought for a moment: 'If you take T, O, S, T, I and V out of "stay positive", you get …'

'Say pie?'

'OK – pie.'

'What?'

'I'm not sure. I'm tired.'

'Listen, I have to go, but good luck *[nickname hidden, too cute]*[25] … and don't forget to bring me back something from Belgium!'

'I've already got you something. It's nothing big, but it is *very* hilarious. I read somewhere that women like hilarious gifts.'

'Hilarious GIFs. We like hilarious GIFs. Cats falling off stuff, men being accidentally punched in the junk by adorable toddlers, that kind of thing.'

'Ah, yes. That was it. Anyway, it's safely stored in my bum bag right now, so …'

'Bum bag?!'

'Yes.'

'You actually *own* a bum bag.'

'No, I only *lease* it,' I said, in a totally sarcastic tone that made me sound like one of the mean girls from the Tina Fey movie *Mean Girls*.

'Well, I think you should *re*lease it, back into the 1980s where it belongs,' replied Anna, quick as a flash. Maybe quicker.

We said goodbye, but only after Anna had once more told me, quite vociferously, to stay put; to leave it until the latest possible moment before I left Philippe's house. I promised her I would do that. I was going to stay right here until a) Philippe showed up, or b) I had to leave to catch my ferry. Whichever came sooner.

* * * * *

My ferry. My ferry came sooner.

* * * * *

Now that I was travelling home empty-handed, I had to admit that this had been an unsuccessful weekend. I sulked the whole way back to Southsea.

. . . .

25 OK, it's 'noodle'. Presumably because I'm white, and big in Japan.

It was pretty tricky to sulk *and* drive across Belgium and into France, as I was pretty busy concentrating on the sat-nav instructions, but sulking on the ferry was easy, as there was nothing to distract me and someone else was steering.

In the on-ship shop, I found those incredibly cheap but fun polystyrene World War II model airplanes with the little propellers on the front for sale. I bought a few Spitfires and Hurricanes and my mood temporarily lifted. But in the main, it was a sulky trip. If I was going to sum it up, I would say it went like this: sulking, happiness at finding some war-related toys, then more sulking.

My leads had all dried up. Scott Minto remained impossible to contact, ditto Lars Bohinen. Keith Curle and Notts County were still in the play-off hunt in League 1, so I was no closer to meeting him either. I had no right to expect to just show up at Philippe Albert's address and find him there, but I was still miffed. For the first time since I had started this little mission, I had stalled.

The following morning, I was due to work for Rosh, from home. And I did, nominally. He sent me some e-mails, I responded. He asked me to do some work, I did it. I wrote some puns for a printers, some copy for a coffee company, and some taglines for a tattooist.

He was happy with the results. But I, on the other hand, was in my pants, and in my bed, and in a bad mood. At some point in the day, I got out of the first two. I stayed in the third all day.

I spoke to Ed, briefly, via telephone. He called to check how my weekend had gone, and I gave him the abridged version of events.

'Stay positive,' he said.

'If you take T, O, S, T, I and V out of "stay positive", then you get …'

'Tostiv?'

'No, say pie,' I said.

'Pie,' replied Ed.

'Forget it.'

'Anyway listen,' he said. 'I went back to my parents' house this weekend. Guess what I found …'

I guessed it would have something to do with Henry VIII.

'Henry VIII's codpiece?' I said.

'No.'

'Henry VIII's suit of armour?'

'No.'

'Henry VIII's …'

'Stickers!'

'His stickers?! Was there a *Wives of Henry VIII* collection?'

'Loads of stickers! And albums!'

'Because that would be six stickers, too.'

'*Premier League 94, 95* and *96*! And some wrestling ones.'

'Really?'

'Really. I've got loads of spare Brutus the Barber Beefcakes.'

This was potentially great news. If Ed had found any of my missing four, I could be on the fast-track to sticker book success.

'Are any of them … ?'

'I haven't checked them all yet. But I don't think so. But I wouldn't give them to you anyway.'

'What? Why not?'

'That would go against the spirit of this whole quest. I couldn't just *give* you the stickers. It would turn this whole exercise into a joke, a folly, the …'

'Scottish Premier League?'

'I was going to say "the sticker book equivalent of Henry VIII's marriage to Anne of Cleves", actually.'

'Is that a history joke?'

'Very much so, yes.'

That evening, I went round to see Anna at her flat. We ate dinner, and she made me laugh just by virtue of her being there, and being herself. There was some slapstick (she walked into a table), there was some wordplay (she pitched two more excellent *Downton Abbey* spin-offs, *Downton Crabby*[26] and *Downton Tabby*[27]), and there was some deadpan, Steven Wright-esque stuff too (she had made me a cake with the words 'some cake' iced on top).

As we ate some 'some cake' cake, I thought back to the first time I met Anna. Never before had I been so sure, so quickly, that I had met someone brilliant and important. In the three weeks or so I had known her, she had re-emphasised my first impression every four or five seconds.

. . . .

26 A shot-for-shot remake of the original, but everyone has crabs.

27 A shot-for-shot remake of the original, but everyone is a cat.

Spending time with her was exciting and fun. I wanted to see her as often as possible. When I wasn't with her, I thought about her. I wanted to talk to other people about how great she was.

And then I realised it. I realised why that curious churning feeling I had felt when I met Anna, the same one I got whenever I saw her, was so familiar. I was in love with her. It sounds preposterous, but I was ridiculously certain of it. *That* was what that indescribable feeling was.

And then I remembered the last time I had felt anything like it. It was the last time I fell in love. And I know I shouldn't be comparing falling in love with a real, live woman with falling in love with football but I'm absolutely about to do that.

* * * * *

My first Portsmouth match was on Boxing Day in 1991. Huddled up for warmth in the North Stand with the rest of my family – mum, dad, my grandparents and my little brother – we watched as Pompey beat Bristol Rovers 2-0 at Fratton Park.

It was a big day. From the moment I saw the ground's spindly and towering floodlights in the distance, I was overwhelmed into saucer-eyed and slack-jawed silence. From the moment we stepped from Fratton train station, I felt as though my feet barely touched the ground. I was swept forward, a wee boy bobbing along on a rough tide of royal blue shirts, heaving and swelling towards the stadium.

Fratton Park itself was the biggest building I had ever seen. Looking back on it now, I would probably say it was 'an unending monolith of crumbling concrete and uneven iron' or '... an iceberg re-imagined on dry land: for every huge block I could see, there seemed ten times more hidden from view'. Particularly if I was feeling in a pretentious kind of mood and felt the need to show off. But at the time, I'd have probably called it 'big' or 'really, really big'.

I was a panicky kid at the best of times – I had my first panic attack aged eight in the planetarium at Disney World, after the voice-over on the film we were watching announced flippantly that one day, the sun was going to EXPLODE – but this was a more enjoyable kind of nervousness. My heart pumped and pounded in my ears as I twisted through the turnstiles towards my seat. That first glimpse of white lines on green grass made me beam from ear to ear, even as my teeth chattered against the cold and my toes wriggled for warmth in the ends of my trainers.

There seemed to be an urgent momentum to everything happening, and always something new to take in. The smell of frying onions, the hundreds of booming voices singing in unison – a catalogue of new sights, sounds and smells hit me for the first time. It was an overwhelming, five-sense experience.

I felt my stomach loop-de-loop as I looked up at the roof of the stand. I felt the air snap-crackle-and-pop with the electricity of thousands of chattering voices. I opened my pristine programme and for the first time, caught the sickly smell of those shiny pages. All of it was completely addictive. The programme smell probably literally so.

I was silent for most of the afternoon. Whenever Pompey poured towards goal, I stared as thousands of heads, shoulders, knees and toes straightened from their seats in expectation. I listened carefully as the ground spontaneously erupted in song. I heard new words: expressive, immediate, explicit ones, like *[bleep]*, *[bleep]*, *[bleep]*, *[bleep]*, *[bleep]*, *[bleep]* and 'scummer'.

I can't recall any of the actual action that afternoon. To my innocent ears, every chastened 'ooh' and mocking 'aah' reverberated at a deafening 11, which is one more than ten and therefore louder. By the time the final whistle sounded, my pristine programme had been wrung into a nervous bugle, because my first match day had been terrifying and exciting, at an age when the world seemed simplistically divided into one or the other.

I wanted more of it, immediately. And not more football in general, but more Pompey. This was the club for me. This was home. I was in love.

And so it was with Anna. But I didn't tell her all this just yet. It was still early days. Sure, she had made me a cake and was helping me find the half-a-dozen former footballers I needed to complete *Premier League 96*, but I wanted to be doubly, triply sure she felt the same way I did first.

I did, however, remind her that I'd bought her a present back from Belgium. She seemed excited, not so much about the gift itself, but the fact that I had brought it round to her flat in my bum bag.

'Put it on,' she said.

'No.'

'Put in on!'

'No,' I said, putting it on anyway. The buckle slotted into position with a tinny click. Anna looked at me and told me I looked like a 14-year-old Spanish exchange student. She didn't say which one, exactly.

I unzipped (the bum bag) and pulled it out (the postcard). I held it up for Anna to inspect (still the postcard). She looked nonplussed.

'It's some stones. In Belgium. Some Belgian stones. On a postcard. It's …'

'Are they famous?'

'Nope.'

'Oh.'

'It's funny.'

'I don't get it.'

'I got you something else, too.'

I reached back into my bum bag and pulled out the Belgian scratchcard, and the polystyrene Spitfire. Anna said these were the weirdest collection of presents she had ever received. I reminded her that the first gift I ever gave her was a passport-sized photograph of a former Blackburn Rovers winger she had never ever heard of. She agreed that she had mis-spoke.

For a minute or two, she played with her new toys. She assembled her plane and threw it across the room, where it crash-landed into a lampshade. She looked at her postcard for a bit. She scratched her scratchcard until her knees were glittery with silver shavings.

'I've won.'

'Won?'

'The Belgian lottery.'

'You've *won the Belgian lottery?!*'

'Looks like it.'

'How much?'

'Ten.'

'Ten?'

'Million.'
'Ten million Euros?!'
'Ten million Euros.'
'No way!'
'Nah.'
'Oh.'

Anna folded up the scratchcard and placed it neatly inside my wallet. While she was in there, she removed another slip of folded paper, one she clearly recognised, and opened it up. She grabbed a pen from the coffee table in front of us, and began to write on the postcard. After a few seconds, she stopped and reached for her phone. She pressed a few buttons, then appeared to copy a number from the phone to the postcard. When she was finished, she held it up in front of my face.

Dear Philippe,

My name is Adam Carroll-Smith and I am a sports journalist and author based in England. As you can see from this postcard, I was recently in Belgium and have plans to return soon. I was wondering – might we be able to arrange a face-to-face interview, the next time I am in the country? My number is 07545XXXXXX. Hope to hear from you soon.

Many thanks,
Adam.

She whisked it away from my face, placed it neatly inside her bag and before I could say 'what are you doing, I can't send Philippe Albert a postcard bought from a shop less than a mile from his house! And how have you managed to forge my signature so accurately?', Anna told me she would post it the following morning.

Speaking of post, Anna handed me the letter which had arrived for me at her flat. I opened it. There was only one thing, a sticker – a Peter Atherton sticker, to be precise – inside. Someone, I had no idea who, had sent me a sticker I didn't need – a swapsie, and not even a very good one.

'Well, what is it?' asked Anna.

'Junk,' I said, chucking it in the bin.

Art, 3

GOAL POST.

(EXTREME CLOSE-UP)

Ten

A FEW DAYS passed – long enough for the postcard to have reached Philippe *en Belgique* – and for a week or so, I allowed my heart to leap with excitement every time my mobile rang. But it was never Philippe Albert. Neither *the* nor *a* Philippe Albert. Most of the time it was Anna ringing to ask if *a* Philippe Albert or *the* Philippe Albert had called. Rosh called a lot, normally to tell me to hurry up and finish my work.

It was May Day, and I was beginning to wish I had planned this whole sticker album thing better. I had no plan of attack. I was bouncing from idea to idea like a [*noun*] [*verb*] in a [*noun*][28]. But it was too late to start being organised now. By the time I got myself sorted, I might have missed countless opportunities to find my final four. I would just have to keep plugging away.

So I did. I spent hours rooting through the internet for interviews with Scott Minto, e-mailing or tweeting the journalists responsible for the write-ups, begging for assistance. I found his agents' website and e-mailed them too. I decided to send Lars Bohinen a tweet a day until he replied. I told him I was writing a book and I needed to talk to him. At the time I *wasn't* writing a book: I was trying to do something that might one day become a book. But that was more than 140 characters.

Ahead of their final games of the season, I re-e-mailed Notts County's press officer Ralph Shepherd and reminded him I still wanted to meet Keith Curle once the season was over. I told him,

· · · · · · ·

28 Sorry, too lazy to think of a simile. And too lazy, in fact, to even finish this sentence with a full stop

quite desperately and totally inaccurately, that I was able to travel to Nottingham 'any time of the week'.

And I decided I needed an insurance policy when it came to meeting Philippe Albert. I still had faith that the whole turning-up-at-his-house/sending-him-a-postcard thing would *eventually* work out, but I needed back-up. His landline was still going unanswered. Nobody was home. I was starting to wonder if anyone ever would be. I found a few journalists who had interviewed him in the past, and sent begging tweets and e-mails.

For a few days after all that plugging, nothing happened. Stuff happened, obviously, but not much relating to this. For example, I noticed my beard had grown a bit too long, but then I trimmed it back to its normal length before anyone saw and no-one was any the wiser.

I went to the gym once too, did eight minutes of exercise, realised it was boring, then sat in the cafe watching some episodes of *The Larry Sanders Show* until I had expunged the memory of those eight minutes treading mill.

That was the period from the end of April until 4 May. On 5 May, a few things happened. Big(ish) things. I don't keep a diary, but if I did, then this is what mine would have looked like.

* * * * *

5 May, 2012
Sunday

1000 hrs
Check e-mails. (Actually, woke up first, then checked e-mails.) Four new messages.

Two very forward messages promising 'opportunities to grow'. *Deleted* (fingers burned before. Wise to the scams now).

One from Anna. *Private.*

One with '*Scott Minto*' in the subject line. A reply from Scott's agents. *Hooray.* They are keen to hear more about why I want to meet him, but are happy to help put me in touch with him once they know a little more about my sticker book project. Disproportionately happy to hear someone refer to this nonsense as a 'project'. Send an uncharacteristically professional reply. Cross fingers for luck and click send.

1020 hrs
Put bread in toaster.

1025 hrs
Check Twitter account. No tweets from Lars Bohinen, so re-send yesterday's tweet. Wait five minutes. No reply. Say 'dang it' to self, loudly. Check Twitter DMs. Two new replies – both from chaps called Richard I had contacted the previous day.

> 1: *Richard Martin (Richard #1)* – Has interviewed Scott Minto recently. Still in touch with him via e-mail. Suggests I write an e-mail to Scott explaining why I want to meet him. He will forward it on.

> 2: *Richard Edwards (Richard #2)* – Has interviewed Philippe Albert before, about to interview him again. Still has his mobile number somewhere, and will send it on soon. Confirms Philippe is a 'great bloke'.

1045 hrs
Write e-mail to Scott and send it to Richard #1 for forwarding. Send reply to Richard #2 and thank him for the help. I am now (almost) in contact with two more of my missing players. Punch air victoriously. Air doesn't punch back. I win.

1100 hrs
Period of extended sitting around. Toilet breaks at regular intervals. Make mental note to get it fixed. Make second mental note to improve pun work.

1500 hrs
Notts County vs. Colchester kicks off. The Magpies need to win to have any chance of getting into the play-offs.

1550 hrs
Notts County are 3-0 up. But Stevenage, the team above them in the final play-off spot (on goal difference) are also winning.

1600 hrs
Remember toast is still in toaster. Relieved it has not been toasting all this time.

1601 hrs
Toast cold. Still eat it.

1655 hrs
Full-time: Notts County are 4-1 winners over Colchester, but miss out on League 1 play-off place on goal difference to Stevenage.

1656 hrs
E-mail Ralph Shepherd, press officer at Notts County. Remind him that I am still keen to meet Keith Curle. Tell him I am 'in Nottingham a lot' in the coming weeks, even though I am not.

1657 hrs
Wonder if I should have waited more than eight or nine seconds after the final whistle before e-mailing Ralph. Bit rude.

1900 hrs
Dinner with Anna. Check Twitter. No reply from Lars. Tell Anna about the toast mix-up. No laugh. Tough crowd. Drive home.

2300 hrs
Realise I haven't uncrossed my fingers. Uncross them. Bed.

* * * * *

6 May 2012
Monday

0830 hrs
Get out of bed (mine). Put clothes on (mine). Pretend I'm trapped in a see-through box (mime).

0835 hrs
Start commute.

0838 hrs

End commute. Working from home. Delayed temporarily in corridor by an unexpected small box. No name or address on it. Remember closing scene from *Seven*. Leave it unopened.

0930 hrs

Check e-mails. Three new messages.

One very blunt message promising 'opportunities to grow'. *Read it* (still a bit curious).

One from Mum. *Private* (for different reasons).

One from Ralph Shepherd, Notts County. *Hooray*. He has spoken to Keith Curle, and Keith Curle is happy to speak to me. He encloses Keith's mobile number. I am delighted. Punch the [*bleep*] out of the air. Feel like driving around town honking my horn (car's horn) and shouting Keith Curle's name. Feel like cartwheeling naked down the street wearing a home-made Keith Curle mask.

0931 hrs

Only do about half of those things in the end. (Can't really cartwheel.)

1000 hrs

Phone call. Rosh checking in from the office. Convince myself he has heard my celebrating all the way in London and become suspicious of my happiness.

1100 hrs

Break. Listen to Electrelane, listen to Surfer Blood, listen to Twilight Sad, listen to Best Coast, in pathetic attempt to crowbar my musical taste into my diary and curry favour with the football hipster fraternity. Also listen to ELO. Put bread in toaster.

1200 hrs

Check Twitter. No reply from Lars Bohinen to yesterday's tweet. Re-send standard message, telling him about the 'book' I am 'writing' and asking him to follow me. Decide, for some reason, to add an exclamation mark today. Immediately regret it. Remember how much I hate exclamation marks.

1223 hrs
A REPLY FROM LARS BOHINEN! A tweet from the Norwegian Zidane! Decide I like exclamation marks after all!!!

1224 hrs
General whooping and air-punching! Practise cartwheels!

1230 hrs
Send Lars Bohinen a direct message (four, actually) explaining sticker book project. Tell him I will be in Norway soon (lie) and would love to interview him face-to-face (true) and promise the coffees will be on me (probably a lie too). Return to senses, RE: exclamation marks.

1300 hrs
Period of unexpected productivity begins.

1600 hrs
Period of unexpected productivity ends.

1602 hrs
End of working day (unofficially).

1700 hrs
End of working day (officially).

1701 hrs
Pick up the box in the hallway. Realise it is way too light to contain a head. Notice my name is actually on the box.

1702 hrs
Open the box. Still thinking about scene from *Seven*. Check thoroughly for heads.

1703 hrs
FULL OF HEADS.

1704 hrs
There are dozens of stickers inside. At first glance, just old,

useless stickers. Eddie McGoldricks, Gavin Peacocks, Rufus Brevetts. That sort of thing.

1715 hrs

Oh [*bleep*]. A missed call, from Belgium. Return the call, no answer.

1715 hrs

Call Anna and tell her what has just happened. 'Oh [*bleep*],' she says. Tell her I said the same thing. Tell her about the random box of stickers. She tells me I was brave to open it and asks me if I've ever seen *Seven.*

1720 hrs

My phone is ringing! It is a Belgian number! And not in the way 'Much Against Everyone's Advice' by Soulwax is a 'Belgian number'. I mean a Belgian *telephone* number! Decide to temporarily abandon this diary shtick for a bit, and get back to more conventional story-telling.

* * * * *

As my phone vibrated in the palm of my hand, I allowed myself a split-second to daydream. I imagined my postcard dropping through Philippe Albert's letterbox. I [*synonym for 'imagined'*] him picking it up off the *bienvenue* mat and reading it, a wry smile spreading across his lips as he is charmed by my *naivety* and enthusiasm. And then I [*another synonym for 'imagined'; probably* 'visualised'] Philippe picking up the phone and calling me.

'Hello?' I said, answering the phone.

'Hello, Adam?' The voice was a deep and peculiar mix of English and French.

'Philippe?'

'Yes.'

'Philippe Albert?'

'Yes.'

'Oh wow, thank you *so* much for …'

'So, you want to brush my moustache, yes?'

'Sorry?'

'Vous aimez brosser moustaches?'

'I don't ...'

'Oui?'

'Er, well, no, but ...'

He exploded into fits of giggles: 'You know it's *not* Philippe Albert, right? It's Jay.'

'Of course,' I lied.

'Get the package OK?'

'I think so. Did you send a letter too? Did you send me stickers?'

'No, I sent you a severed head. Have you seen *Seven*?'

'Er ...'

'It was a package. Stickers, yeah. Have you been through them yet?'

'Not yet.'

'Do it now.'

'But we're on the phone. Won't this be boring?'

'No, I'll wait.'

'Are you sure? The FA Cup Final is on.'

'This will be less boring.'

I thumbed my way through the pile, saying the names of the stickers aloud as I did. There was Earl Barrett, John Jensen, Mark Hateley, the bottom half of a Liverpool player on a neon background, a Blackburn shiny, Mark Hateley, a Nottingham Forest programme, Tommy Widdrington, Mark Hateley, Peter Atherton (again), Teddy Sheringham, Henning Berg, Steve Watson, Mark Hateley, Manchester United team photo, Mark Hateley, (not yet Sir) Alex Ferguson, Graeme Souness, Mark Hateley, and so and so on. Most of them were the wrong year, either a year or two too early or a few years too late.

I told Jay the bad news. He sounded disappointed and I immediately felt guilty. He had probably spent time and effort going through old boxes of his childhood possessions to find these, and here I was, telling him they were essentially useless.

'They might come in handy,' I said. 'For swaps.'

'Maybe,' he said, quite dejectedly.

'Seriously, thanks so much for sending them to me,' I added, with the enthusiasm of an average American working in the service industry. It seemed to do the trick. Jay perked up, and told me he would be over in England for the weekend starting 18 May. I told him to give me a call. I found an elastic band, tied it round the stickers and threw them in my bag.

The following morning, I called Keith Curle. I explained my sticker book mission. I told him I needed to meet him as soon as possible so I could take his picture and fill his gap in the album. You know, the normal stuff you say to a former England centre-half who you've spent the past few months madly trying to track down.

We got our respective diaries out and compared our availability. I was freer than he was, but Keith said he could squeeze me into his schedule any time from 28 May onwards. I jumped at the chance and told him I was free on the 28th. It was a Monday, which meant I almost certainly wouldn't be free, but that wasn't important right now. Rosh would only be upset if he found out what I was up to. I decided I would make sure he didn't find out what I was up to. I told Ed though. He promised he could keep my trip a secret and maybe even run interference if Rosh started getting suspicious.

I booked my train tickets and my motorway hotel with scenic views of the mid-1970s immediately, and reflected on a truly excellent couple of days. In a week's time, I had a meeting with sticker number three, all booked up and pencilled – penned, indelibly, more like – into my diary. Which we've already established doesn't actually exist.

Lars Bohinen was now following me on Twitter. Scott Minto's agents had given me the green light to meet him, more or less, and even if they didn't, Richard #1 had forwarded him my e-mail, which might cut out the middle-men altogether. Philippe Albert had not yet replied to my postcard, nor answered his home telephone, but Richard #2 was going to forward me his mobile number any day now.

Things were going well. That much should be obvious. For the past two months, I had spent every (i.e. *a lot of*) minute(s), of every (i.e. *most*) day(s) e-mailing and tweeting and calling and searching for my missing stickers. Now the hard work was beginning to pay off.

Of course, I should have felt happy. But I didn't. I felt sad, miserable, dejected. Whichever is worst.

Wait: sorry, I mistyped.

I *was* happy. I should have felt happy and I *did* feel happy. I felt the very opposite of miserable. I was delighted, ecstatic, priapic. Maybe not *that* happy, actually, but if I had to summarise my feelings, I would say I was very, *very* satisfied. I hope I'm making that clear.

* * * * *

0930 hrs
I am on a diet. No, a train. I am on a train. Man sitting opposite me playing really intricate air guitar – he tuned up, he clipped a capo on, he moved his air guitar away from his air amplifier because he was getting a bit of feedback. He looks almost exactly like Owen Coyle.

0935 hrs
Train stops at a station. Not sure which station. My money is on 'train'. Watch a small dog eating an Upper Crust sandwich like a human (holding it between two paws, standing on its hind legs). I am miles from Sheffield. I am going to be late for my meeting with Keith Curle. Air guitar man still going. *Really* looks like Owen Coyle.

0940 hrs
Ticket collector comes around. Like most ticket inspectors, he looks exactly like Roy Evans. I frantically fumble about for my ticket in my trouser pockets. Look down. I am not wearing any trousers.

0945 hrs
Wake up.

0946 hrs
Wake up a bit more. No sign of Owen Coyle, Roy Evans or that dog eating a sandwich like a human. Realise my meeting with Keith Curle isn't for another few weeks. Realise that, therefore, I am not running late for meeting with Keith Curle.

1015 hrs
Head into town for some breakfast with Anna.

1100 hrs
Eat toast. Eat eggs. Eat tea (drink). Finish breakfast.

1105 hrs
Bill arrives. 'Hi Bill,' I say. Waiter brings the food bill over shortly after. Looks exactly like Bruce Rioch. The waiter, not the food bill. Fumble about in my pockets for my wallet. Look down. I am not wearing any trousers.

1106 hrs
Mark Hateley.

Jokes, 22–24.

Hannover 96 – 1899 Hoffenheim. (A big away win.)

Stadium designers! Confuse no-nonsense defenders. Change Row Z to Row 26.

The terms of Jens Lehmann's contracts were always *very* simple.

Eleven

FOR THE next few weeks, I decided to grow my beard. I had a beard already, but I decided to grow it even more. While I counted down the days (nine) until I was due to meet Keith Curle in Sheffield, my schedule was pretty consistent: I worked during the week, hung out with Anna every evening and cultivated my beard.

All I had to do was not shave it, but I had to not do that every day. That took discipline. On more than one occasion (two occasions) I found myself poised to shave and had to physically restrain myself from spoiling my hard work. It is difficult to physically restrain yourself, but I did it. I had to. I resisted, but eventually I learned my lesson.

Work was boring, but work had been a bit boring for a little while. Truthfully, I felt as though I had hit a wall, career-wise. I wasn't unhappy, but I wasn't having a ball either. While my friends were just now beginning to really advance in their careers, I was stagnating.

Things with Anna, however, were going really well. She remained ridiculously excited about the prospect of me finishing my sticker album. I remained convinced I was in love with her, but too frightened to tell her. I hoped she might interpret my bushier beard as a subtle declaration of my true feelings, but she didn't. That was probably my fault. I was being too vague. I still wasn't brave enough to be honest with her. That still felt like too mature a thing to do.

She had, though, taken to scratching the hair under my chin like I was a dog. That had to be a good sign. At the very least, she loved me like a pet. Sure, nobody wants to date their dog, but nobody is ever going to sit their dog down and say 'I don't love you' to them either. It was a start.

Jay was in London, so I travelled up from Southsea to meet him for a few beers. Another letter arrived for me at Anna's flat, presumably from him again, containing another Peter Atherton sticker. It was obviously his idea of a joke. He had clearly been in Belgium too long if it was. I didn't mention it. If he knew I didn't get the joke – and that I had summarily binned the sticker on both occasions – he might be offended. I am nice like that.

I called Ed and asked him if he wanted to come for a drink too. He said, 'Was Henry VIII's father the Lancastrian Henry Tudor who defeated the Yorkist King Richard III at the Battle of Bosworth Field on August 22nd 1485?' Then he laughed and put the phone down. I did some Googling and realised that was his way of saying yes.

The three of us met, coincidentally, in Rosh's local in east London. The pub was empty, save for the same few weathered regulars propping up the bar. John Cale's '4'33"' was still playing on the jukebox, but Ed said it sounded like nothing, and put back-to-back-to-back-to-(etc) Doobie Brothers on instead. Jay went to the bar and brought back three beers.

Jay and Ed got along well. They had a mutual interest in being liked by people they had only just met, and a firm interest in swelling their number of Facebook friends and Twitter followers. We talked about everything important (politics, relationships, music, film, football, blimps, foxy boxing) and everything unimportant too (football stickers).

We should have spent longer on the important things. But instead, we mainly talked football stickers. I showed Ed the rubber-banded bunch of stickers that Jay had sent me through the post. Jay looked proud and pleased. Ed shrugged. He looked quite impressed, at best.

'I'm *quite* impressed,' he said, confirming my earlier hunch.

'I was just thinking that,' I replied.

'*Quite* impressed? Look at that pile! It's massive!' said Jay. 'They were in one of the boxes of my "childhood memories" at my parents' house in Amsterdam. It took me ages to find them too …'

'No, no,' said Ed. 'It's good. It's just not quite ...' he disappeared below the table and into his bag. Not literally. He just dipped his head below the table and reached into his bag with his hand. After a few seconds, he re-surfaced. He slapped something down on the table.

Thud.

It was very big.

It was very impressive.

It was the largest I had seen in years, no question.

It was another ambiguous description that gives you the impression a very large human penis had just landed with a thud on our table (it hadn't).

It was a triple double-banded stack of hundreds of stickers. It looked a little bit like my long-lost adoptive brother, Sticky. I asked him how his parliamentary career was going and he ignored me. I leaned closer and told him I thought Britain's continued membership of the EU was a good thing, but he didn't react. False alarm. This was not Sticky.

'That ... is ... ridiculous!' said Jay. 'Amazing!'

'But ... how? And ... where?' I asked.

'Like Jay said,' replied Ed. 'In my parents' loft. In a box marked 'ED', with five exclamation marks. And there's more ...'

Ed vanished back below deck and back into his rucksack. After a few seconds, he bobbed back up with something else in his hands. He slapped it down on the table.

It was big.

It was shiny.

It was 12 inches long, maybe longer.

It was another ambiguous description that gives you the impression a very large robot penis had just landed with a thud on our table (it hadn't).

It was a copy of *Premier League 96.*

'That ... is ... even *more* ridiculous,' said Jay. 'And even *more* amazing!'

'Is it finished?' I asked.

Ed said nothing.

'Is it?' asked Jay.

Ed continued to say nothing. He opened the album to the Sheffield Wednesday page. Two gaps (sadly, he already had

Peter Atherton, so Jay, who apparently had an unlimited supply, couldn't help). He turned to the Newcastle and Wimbledon pages. One gap each. He showed us the Coventry, Arsenal, and Southampton pages. Three more gaps apiece. Across the Bolton pages, he was four shy, including the shirt shiny.

I had been keeping score on my fingers. By my calculations, Ed was an even ten short. Jay pointed out that the actual number was 17 and that I had just run out of fingers. I checked. He was right.

Ed picked up his stack of stickers, and loosened the rubber bands. He began to fan the stickers out. After a few seconds, he stopped searching, pulled out a single sticker and put it on the table, midway between us.

'Lars Bohinen,' he said.

'So it is,' I replied, trying to sound as though I was unmoved. But I wasn't unmoved. I was moved. In fact, I was moved to pick it up and hold it in my hands. I did that thing you sometimes see in romantic comedies, where someone strokes the face in the picture. It was a weird thing to do. Ed snatched it back from me.

'Obviously I can't just give this to you.'

'Obviously. Hold on: why not?'

'I've told you this already. I can't give it to you, because that's not how this works. This is supposed to be a challenge, right?'

'Right.'

'Because otherwise, it'd be too easy. It'd be a joke, a folly, a waste of time …'

'The Scottish Premier League, yes, we all know how that bit goes now.'

'Right.'

'So what do we do now?' I asked.

'We do what we did as children. We get our swapsies out.'

* * * * *

FADE IN.

INT. PUB BACK ROOM – NIGHT

THE ROOM is dimly lit. In the centre of the room is a pool table, covered over with a wooden board. The wooden floor is covered in dust. Faded photographs in dust-covered gold frames line the walls. There are three small tables, each with three chairs around them, in the corners of the room. At one table sits ADAM, ED and JAY.

Some music – 'LISTEN TO THE MUSIC' by THE DOOBIE BROTHERS – is playing. The only other sound is the occasional clink of glasses, the quiet rattling of pipes and the scraping of chairs on the wooden floor.

ADAM
Who do you need?

ED
Who do you have?

ADAM
Just tell me who you need.

ED
Just tell me who you have.

ADAM
Fine. Earl Barrett?

ED
Got.

ADAM
John Jensen.

ED
Got.

ADAM
Mark Hateley.

ED
Got.

ADAM
Are you sure?

ED
Yes.

ADAM
I've got about 50.

ED
I don't need him.

ADAM
Fine. Tommy Widdrington, Teddy Sheringham, Henning Berg.

ED
Got. Got. Got.

ADAM
Steve Watson, Alan Wright, Glenn Helder.

ED
Got. Got. Got.

ADAM
Barry Horne.

ED
Got.

ADAM
Erik Thorstvedt.

ED
Got.

ADAM
Eddie McGoldrick.

ED
Need!

ADAM
Really?!

ED
Nah. Got.

ADAM
That's not funny.

JAY
It's *pretty* funny.

ADAM
Steve Lomas?

ED
OK, *seriously*, need. I need him!

ADAM
This isn't funny, Edward.

ED
I'm serious. I need him!

ADAM
(sighs)
Seriously?

ED
Nah. Got.

JAY laughs so much that his head falls off and rolls under the pool table. We discover that JAY is in fact a highly-sophisticated and human-realistic robot.

ADAM
I'm not going to carry on if you keep doing this.

ED
Sorry. I'll behave.

ADAM
Darren Peacock.

ED
Got.

ADAM
Dmitri Kharine.

ED
Got. And that's a *Premier League 94* sticker.

ADAM
Spurs shiny, Liverpool shiny, John Lukic, Nottingham Forest Programme ...

ED
Got, got, got, got.

ADAM
Are you sure I can't tempt you with a Mark Hateley or two?

ED
No.

ADAM
Fine. Carl Tiler?

ED
Carl *Tiler*?!

ADAM
Carl Tiler.

ED
Carl Tiler!

ED stands up and reaches across the desk. He snaps the sticker from ADAM's hand. When he sees the sticker, ED laughs riotously and punches the air. He begins to run around the room. He kicks JAY's head in celebration. It crashes into the wall and a picture of some dogs playing poker wobbles and crashes to the floor. ED returns to the table, and sits down. He is smiling. A lot.

ADAM
So … Carl Tiler, then.

ED stares at the sticker intensely. He shakes his head, in apparent disbelief, then puts the sticker back on the table.

ED
Got.

ADAM
What?

ED
Did you know Henry VIII was 6ft 4in?

ADAM
What do you mean, 'got'?

ED
Oh. I've got him. I don't need Carl Tiler.

ADAM
But you just ran around the room! You punched the air! You kicked Jay's head!

ED
I know.

ADAM
WHY?!

ED
(shrugging)
I just like Carl Tiler.

ADAM
That's not funny.

JAY
(OFF CAMERA)
It's *pretty* funny.

ADAM pushes JAY's headless body off his chair. It lands with a loud and metallic thud.

ADAM
(sighing)
Paul Warhurst ...

ED
Got.

FADE OUT.

I eventually made it through the whole stack of stickers Jay had donated. Ed didn't need any of them. He only repeated what he was now calling 'The Carl Tiler Manoeuvre' seven or eight more times. Each time I found it less funny, and Jay found it more funny. His head didn't really fall off, by the way. That was an over-exaggeration. He might be a robot though. I haven't checked. I'll try and find out for you by the end of this book.

At the end of the night, Ed took me to one side – starboard, I think – and told me he really wanted to just give me the Lars Bohinen sticker, but he couldn't. He handed me a piece of paper. On it was a list of the 17 stickers he needed to complete his album. He told me if I could find any of them, he would gladly swap with me.

I looked at it and noticed that one of them was Stig-Inge Bjørnebye. I told Ed I had a photograph of a man who worked with Stuart Ripley who looked a *lot* like him. He said that didn't count.

'Do I need to *meet* the players on this list?' I asked.

'No. If you can find an original sticker, I'll take that too. But I've been trawling through eBay for a few days now and I can't find them. Maybe meeting them would be easier. I mean, you've met two of your six already, and the other four are more or less in the bag, right? You're good at this. You have a talent for it.'

'A talent for meeting former Premier League footballers?'

'It's something.'

I nodded. Ed, Jay and I said our goodbyes, and I caught the last train back to Southsea. I checked my e-mails and my Twitter account. Neither Scott Minto nor his agents/managers/whoever they were had replied to my e-mails. Richard #2 hadn't yet sent through Philippe Albert's mobile number. And worst of all, Lars Bohinen was no longer following me on Twitter. And that could only mean one thing. He had received the private messages I had sent him, the ones explaining my sticker book project, and had come to the (highly logical) conclusion that I was an idiot.

A few days previously, it had seemed as though Lars was in the bag. A few hours earlier, his sticker had literally been in my hands. But now he, and Scott and Philippe too, felt a million miles away. Or however many miles Norway + Belgium + probably somewhere near London added up to.

* * * * *

28 May 2012
Monday

My hotel room was small and clean. Like Ronnie Corbett. The sky outside was big and blue and not very funny. Like Roy Chubby Brown. I tried to compare the bathroom, carpet, furniture and kettle to some other old comedians, but I couldn't think of any more so I abandoned that little conceit. From my window, I could see a few noisy rails of train line, a busy main road and a set of four car tyres lying by the side of the road. An old bumper and two

131

rusty wing-mirrors were lying by the side of the road too. And some windscreen wipers and – actually, it was just a complete old car, parked up by the side of the road.

I had a few hours to fill until my meeting with Keith Curle. We had agreed the previous evening to meet in a Starbucks near his house at 10am, and it was barely 8.30am.

I opened my laptop and checked for any e-mails from Rosh. None so far. As far as he knew, I was sat at home in Southsea, just an hour-and-a-bit away from London, working away diligently on whatever it was I had promised I would work away diligently on the previous week.

I called Anna. She had just started work, and she was busy baking a Bakewell tart when I rang. Which was weird, because bakery isn't usually a big part of being a knee surgeon. Then I remembered she wasn't a knee surgeon but a chef and a master-baker, and the cake-baking made sense.

I asked her if she had anything she would like to ask Keith Curle ('no'), and told her I would bring her back a souvenir, as was now our custom (so far: a passport-sized picture of Stuart Ripley, a Belgian postcard/lottery ticket, a polystyrene WWII model plane, and a biscuit from Gary Penrice's house). She wished me good luck. Both with the meeting, and in choosing my souvenir.

I found the Starbucks near Keith's house where we had arranged to meet, and took a seat in a quiet corner near the back. I was early, and I had forgotten to bring my portable mp3 music player (or pmmp, as I call it), which meant that I had time to think. Maybe too much time to think, which was potentially troublesome.

The last time I had too much time to think about something – where to do a work placement while I was at university – I ended up working in Basingstoke. For free. Another time, I ended up locking myself out my own house because I wanted to see whether the front door was locking properly. It was. I had to watch the second half of a Merseyside derby through my own window.

But before my imagination could run too far away with me, the door to Starbucks swung open. I recognised the man walking through it immediately. In fact, he seemed to have barely aged a day in the past two decades, a slight grey tinge to his hair the only real difference. He still looked like a professional footballer.

He shuffled his way through the shop, stopping briefly to shake hands with someone, presumably a fan or maybe just a really tactile man with a hand fetish.

Eventually, he found his way to my table. I stood up and introduced myself, and Keith Curle – sticker number 435, the third of my missing six – shook my hand. And I relaxed, because unless I did something really mental in the next few minutes, I was about to take my sticker album from a paltry 99.25 per cent complete to an impressive (but still not quite good enough) 99.43 per cent complete.

Keith and I made some nondescript small-talk – respective distances travelled to get here, traffic, weather, Richard Nixon's legacy on American presidential politics, the usual – and as we did, I got the impression Keith didn't quite know what he was about to let himself in for. Though that was mainly because he had just asked me, quite suspiciously, what he had let himself in for.

So I explained everything. I told Keith about who I had met already and who I still had to track down. At the mention of the name 'Gary Penrice', Keith smiled.

'I know Penny,' he said.

'Yeah, he mentioned. He said you've been friends since childhood.'

'That's true. But then *everyone* was friends with Penny back then. He was very popular. Always had a *lot* of mates.'

'Well, he's a very nice man,' I said, accurately.

'Yeah he is. Good old Penny. But that wasn't why he was so popular …'

Now, I could tell you now why Gary Penrice was so popular, but I won't.

Instead, I will build suspense and end this chapter on a cliff-hanger.

Like the film *Cliffhanger*.

* * * * *

Actually, I'll just tell you now. You're probably busy. You might be about to get off the train and head to work, and if I don't tell the secret to Gary Penrice's childhood popularity now, you'll be distracted at your desk until lunch. Your mind will be racing. You might get a telling-off from your boss, and I don't want to be responsible for that. I don't want to be a dick about this.

'So why *was* Gary Penrice so popular?' I asked.

Keith smiled. 'Because his mum was *stunning*.'

'His mum …?'

'… was *stunning*.'

'And so … ?'

'So everyone wanted to go back to Penny's house after school.'

So now you know. According to Keith Curle, Gary Penrice's mum was a very beautiful young woman. As Keith told me, I couldn't help put picture a pint-sized Keith Curle gazing lovingly at Gary Penrice's mum as she poured them both a cold glass of lemonade. And I imagined a pre-teen Gary Penrice scowling at him across the kitchen, his moustache trembling with anger.

Jokes, 25–27.

Unnecessarily pundit-centric jokes about people who are probably lovely chaps and for which I apologise in advance.

Did you hear about the time Mark Lawrenson found joy and meaning in something he saw on a football pitch? Me neither.

The longest sentence ever recorded in the English language is always the one Garth Crooks is about to start on *Football Focus*.

What's the difference between Robbie and Lily Savage? One is a platinum-haired and fake-tanned drag act who knows nothing about football, and the other one…*etc etc etc.*

Twelve

WE TALKED briefly about Keith's career. After starting at his home-town team Bristol Rovers, he moved to Torquay, then back to Bristol to play for City. From there, he joined Reading, spent three years at 'Crazy Gang' era Wimbledon, and then became the joint most expensive defender in British football by moving to Manchester City in 1991.

After five years, he moved to Wolves, where he stayed for four years, until he left to join Neil Warnock for two years at Sheffield United as a player-coach. From Bramall Lane, he moved to Barnsley and then shortly after, Mansfield, where he became player-manager for three years, until 2005. He lost his hyphen when he became boss at first Chester, then Torquay, before being reunited with Neil Warnock at Crystal Palace, where he worked as a coach. He followed Colin to QPR, then became Notts County boss in 2012.

I showed Keith *Premier League 96*. I pointed him towards the gap where his face should have been. And for the third time in just under two months, I told a former Premier League star the whole story of my 16-year-old sticker album, and my plan to meet and photograph the six players missing from it. He told me it was a funny idea. I didn't bother to check if he meant 'funny, ha ha' or 'funny, weird'. I was already pretty certain what he meant.

'A lot has changed since your playing days, hasn't it?' I said.

'Everything has changed, in football,' he replied. 'Besides the obvious things, like the money and the finance, I even think things like the atmosphere around football clubs is less welcoming than it was. Football clubs are more stressful places to work, certainly.

KEITH CURLE

'For example, at QPR, in the season after we got promoted to the Premier League, the changing room suddenly became a lot less welcoming. The players became more selfish – there was more pressure on them now they were in the Premier League and they thought about themselves more; about getting themselves in the starting line-up first, and then worrying about the team. That made the banter go from the dressing room. The spirit went. It was not a nice room, compared to the atmosphere that was in there during the promotion season.

'And that's because the game is more serious now. We definitely had more fun back when I played, than the current players do. We would sit in the hotel bar having a few bottles of beer and then went out to play the next day. You don't get the impression that players have that social stuff anymore.

'There was more of a naivety to the game when I played, too. There were personalities, but no egos. It was just a game of football and that's how most people treated it. The most important thing was just enjoying the game. I remember being a kid, playing in the fourth division, with no agent, not making thousands of pounds and that was enough for me. I never felt any pressure to be successful – even at a massive club like Man City – we just enjoyed the game.

'And it was never about the money. Never. But nowadays, football is *all* about finance. Footballers seem to be more aware that it's a career and that while the rewards are there, they should grab them and make as much as they can. I don't begrudge anyone earning what they can, but it's a big change in the game.

'As a manager, I'm dealing with players earning between £1,000 and £2,000 pounds a week, and they're more street-wise. They have more affordable, real lifestyles. They're more prepared for life; they're more rounded. They think about their mortgages and their pensions and their car payments and that sort of thing.

'But if you're on £50,000 a week, it's easy to live like that money is always going to be there. There will be footballers used to earning that much money *and* spending it too, who will find it very difficult to adjust to not having the limelight and the fame and the money. That's a certainty.

'Depression in football is becoming a bigger issue now, a growing disease, even though the money has gone up and that tells you something. The buzz is bigger and replacing that is difficult. If you can't find it again, you search for it and you can lose your motivation for life. The higher you go, the further you fall.

'Footballers – and football – needs looking after. Nobody is saving for a rainy day, or even just for tomorrow. And that's how football is a bit now – everyone is chasing that promised land, but if they fail, the downside is going to be so much worse.

'That applies to clubs too. The fact the Premier League is called "the promised land" says it all. It's easy to see why clubs are mismanaged trying to get into there, or get *back* there, because it really is this league which is *so* distinct from the rest of the footballing world. It's a place where the money is so huge, that clubs are taking risks to get there. There was always more of a link between the divisions, back in the day, but now the Premier League is almost a separate entity.

'And I think the Premier League has made it harder for fans of lower league clubs to develop an affinity with their team, because the big clubs – the ones who have all the money – can just hoard all the talent. That's made the loan market so important to clubs lower down the pyramid, but also it means there is often a revolving door of players coming in for a few months at a time at almost every smaller club.

'We had eight on loan last season, and five loan players starting the last game of last season a few weeks ago. The quality is getting better down the league, because good players and in particular promising youngsters are being farmed out, but I'm not sure who that benefits.

'The Premier League has also made lower league football more of a short-term thing. We are offering mainly one-year contracts, at most two years with an option for a third if the player is the right age. Clubs – and footballers – below the top league, feel less secure, less permanent. Everyone is more impatient. Football is obsessed with the short-term. But that is the way society is at the moment, too.'

Keith checked his watch. He needed to get away, and I had to get back to pretending to work for Rosh. Keith apologised for not being able to spare me a little more time, but told me to call him if I needed to talk any more. He also told me I should think about writing a book about my sticker album quest. I told him I might.

He said it could be an in-depth look at how the game had changed since 1996, but I told him that had already been done a billion times, by proper football writers who were more interested in facts and research than making jokes about Phil Masinga. He suggested that maybe I could think about writing a book about how I spent a few mad months trying to complete this album. Or I could write one about how my relationship with football had changed, instead.

My *relationship* with football? I told him I would think about it.

* * * * *

That afternoon, in my tiny hotel room in Sheffield, I thought about it. And once I had finished thinking about it, I called Anna.

'I don't know how I didn't realise it sooner,' I said.

'Realise what?' asked Anna.

'What this whole thing has been about. Why I've been so obsessed with completing the sticker album.'

'You've been obsessed because you found an old sticker album that you thought was finished, and realised it wasn't. *That* is why you wanted to complete it – because it was incomplete. It's simple. It doesn't need to be any more complicated than that.'

'But there *is* more to it than that. It's *not* that simple. This has been about something else – my relationship with football.'

'Your *relationship with football*?'

'Yes.'

'What about your *relationship with football*?'

'Are you saying that in italics? I feel like you might be.'

'Nope. Face it, you don't have the knack.'

'Damn. Anyway, my relationship with football has changed,' I said. 'I love football. I really do. But I feel like nowadays, I only love it because I've *always* loved it. I love it, because that's what I've always done. But really, the magic has gone a little bit. Football annoys me.'

I paused, for dramatic effect, and took a deep breath. I could feel a monologue coming on. A searing, brutally honest soliloquy on the way in which money and celebrity and television and Count Blatter had all turned a simple game into a complicated one, an exciting sport into a boring and predictable procession, and mutated its principal participants from rocky-faced everymen into preening prima donnas. You know the sort of thing.

'Are you still there?' said Anna.

I told her I was pausing for dramatic effect and that I was taking a deep breath because I could feel a monologue coming on.

'When I was collecting *Premier League 96* the first time around, football was genuinely exciting,' I said, moving to centre-stage for the start of the aforementioned monologue. It would be really helpful at this point if you could imagine me stood on a stage, a single spotlight illuminating me.

'Even the actual football being played was more thrilling. Take the Newcastle team that Philippe Albert was a part of. They were reckless, and they were attacking. Sure, they were tactically pretty one-dimensional – the plan was to win by scoring one more than the opposition, even if that meant having to score five or six hundred goals – but they were so exciting. I didn't support them, but I wanted to watch them. I wanted to emulate Philippe and Ferdinand and Shearer on the playground at school.'

'Shearer? The moving menswear mannequin from *Match of the Day*?' said Anna, alliteratively.

'Yes, him. My point is that no-one plays like the Newcastle team of 1996 now. The game has moved on tactically and technically, of course, but after talking to Stuart and Gary and Keith, I realise that's not why teams like Newcastle don't exist anymore. It's not just because the standard has improved. It's because the stakes are so much higher. It's because the price of failure is massive now. Let me explain ...'

'Do I have to?' asked Anna.

'... back in 1996, the Premier League was on its way to being the huge deal it is now, but it wasn't quite there yet. Wages were growing, but they weren't yet at the level they are now. Did you know Lee Cattermole earns enough money to buy Canada? The TV rights were sold for big money, but nothing like what they are now. The gap between the Premier League and the rest of football was much, much smaller.

'So what that meant was very simple: if you were a Premier League club and you got relegated, it was *totally* annoying, but it wasn't the end of the world. But now it is. The Premier League is *so* much richer than the rest of British football – it's not so much the top of the football pyramid, as another pyramid altogether – that once you get there, the *only* imperative for most of the clubs is to stay there.

'So unless you're one of the six or seven teams who are pretty much guaranteed not to be relegated every season, you start each year with the same aim – the same incredibly negative target – and that is to *not* get relegated. And when you have thirteen clubs all striving for little more than survival every season, you end up with negative, cagey football.

'You end up losing teams like Newcastle 96. You end up with two teams playing with one striker and two or three thousand defensive midfielders, each trying to catch each other on the break, or nick a goal from a set-piece. NICK! Like scoring a goal is a criminal offence.'

'Which it isn't?'

'No. The game has been robbed of some of its unpredictability. Like for instance, a decade and a half ago, it wasn't always the same teams finishing in the top four. The teams in *Premier League 96* are laid out in the order in which they finished the previous season.

'That year, Nottingham Forest were third in the album and they'd only been promoted *that year*. Arsenal were 12th, behind QPR, Southampton and Wimbledon. A year or two earlier, Aston Villa and Norwich were in the top three. Blackburn got promoted from the second tier, and a few years later they won the title. That kind of thing does not happen anymore.'

'You're rambling quite a bit here,' interrupted Anna.

'I'm usually more lucid than this.'

'I'm just saying that this bit is quite unfocused.'

'Thanks, *Times Literary Supplement*.'

'You are welcome.'

'But anyway: there's so much else that has changed, too. Even the footballers themselves are different. I only need to look through my album to see that. They used to be ugly. They used to be grizzly and rough and full of character. Even David Beckham looks absolutely awful in *Premier League 96*. There is not a whitened tooth or shaped eyebrow in the whole album. They might not have been everymen, but they at least looked familiar and real. None of them look like they lived in six-storey, gold-plated replicas of their own faces, like Nicklas Bendtner probably does.'

'Is that a football joke?'

'Nicklas Bendtner? Yes. Imagine if you crossed the out-of-control ego and deluded sense of self-worth of an average *Apprentice* contestant with the footballing ability of an average *Apprentice* contestant. That's Nicklas Bendtner.'

'OK. Is your monologue over now?'

'Well, I could go on. There's so much to mention.'

'Just give me the headlines. What have you realised? What's the big realisation you've come to?'

'That completing this album is about reconnecting with the simple thrill football gave me as a kid; about remembering that football is a game of romance and adventure and possibilities. That away from all the money talk, TV hype, transfer sagas, greed and corruption and short-termism and ego and ...'

'Stay focused. Are you this rambling in print?'

'Basically, yes. What I'm saying is that I realise this album is symbolic. It's a relic of a better era in football. Maybe the last truly decent one, ever. I want to complete the album, because I want to reconnect with that time and hopefully, by reaching back and touching the past through the players missing from the album, be able to transplant that childish glee and happiness I felt towards football into my current relationship with it.

'If I can work out why football filled me with such joy back then, I figure I might be able to feel that way again. The things that are missing from the game – unpredictability, fun, innocence – are all things that informed my decision to start this sticker album thing in the first place. Does that make sense?'

Anna said nothing for a little while.

'I guess,' she said. 'But are you sure you aren't over-thinking this? Are you sure you're not just *really* annoyed the album isn't finished?'

'Well yes,' I said. 'But like I said: it's about *more* than that.'

'So if you re-discover this mythical childhood love for football before you get all the stickers you need, then you won't mind if you *never* complete the album?'

'Nope. I won't mind,' I said, lying.

'That's bull[*bleep*],' said Anna, not lying.

'No it isn't,' I said, notching up another lie to make it two lies to no lies in my favour.

'So you wouldn't be interested in hearing that I know where Scott Minto lives, for example?'

'You know where Scott Minto lives?!'

'Yes. But I'm not telling you where he lives until you admit that it *is* important that you complete this album.'

'But I just did a big monologue that explains why this sticker album quest is about *more* than just finding the stickers!'

'I know. But I don't agree. So I want you to just admit that the most important thing is completing the album. That first and foremost, this quest has just been about adventure for adventure's sake; about doing something fun and stupid and exciting.'

'Stupid?'

'Stupid.'

I sighed. 'You're right.'

'Hooray. He lives in Orpington.'

'Orpington?'

'That's what is says on the town's Wikipedia page. Gary Rhodes and Dizzee Rascal live there too, apparently.'

'Not together though?'

'Probably not.'

'Well, there's only one way to find out. Fancy a trip to Orpington this weekend?'

'Definitely,' said Anna. 'You've sucked the momentum right out of the story with all this introspective, "why am I doing this?" nonsense. No-one cares. You are missing some stickers, you need to find them, *that's it*. Come on, let's get back on track. We need some more action,' she added, in quite a clever meta sort of way.

I didn't get her a souvenir.

Art, 4

Thirteen

Boooooooop.[29]

. . . .
29 And that makes sixteen. Now we're even.

146

Art, 5.

Fourteen

2 June 2012[30]
Saturday

ANNA AND I set off early on the Saturday morning, with only a loose plan of attack in mind. The previous evening, we had printed out some pictures of Scott Minto, with the words 'HAVE YOU SEEN THIS MAN?' and my mobile number written underneath. After a few glasses of wine, it had seemed like a great idea. In the cold light of day, it seemed like a great idea too. Which meant it must have been a pretty great idea. I asked Anna what she thought of the posters.

'What do you think of these posters?' I asked Anna, as we motored up from Southsea.

'I think they're a *great* idea,' she said.

Satisfied that the posters were a great idea, we headed for Orpington. We got lost for a bit and ended up in Pratts Bottom (pause for laughter), which is a little place quite near Orpington.

After a few minutes of aimless driving, we stopped and told a local we had 'accidentally got ourselves stuck in Pratts Bottom' and we 'needed to know the best way out'. We found a sign with 'Pratts Bottom' written on it and took turns slapping it, and then, after we had got bored of such immature larks (two years later) we drove the three miles up the road to Orpington. I realised that 'Orpington' was an anagram of 'Porno Ting', which I thought Anna would appreciate. It had, after all, been quite a smutty day so far.

. . . .
30 At around about this point, the following [paraphrased] conversation took place with my publishers, 'Hey Adam, we hear you are trying to complete an old football sticker album of yours. Do you feel like writing a book about it?' I told them I did. And now, here we are. Isn't it magical?

But we weren't in Pratts Bottom anymore. The moment had passed. She didn't laugh. I said it a few more times but on each occasion, she weirdly seemed to find it less funny.

We parked up on what looked like a little main road, lined with shops on one side, and a few large pubs on the other. I stuck a poster on the side of one of the pubs, and slipped another under the windscreen of a car. Anna put one in a phone box, and handed another to a man who, judging by the size of his tie knot, sold things to people for a living. We watched as he took it, looked at it, then threw it into a bin.

'We should have printed more than four posters,' said Anna.

'I did. I made five. I think I lost one.'

'I told you it wasn't enough.'

'I thought it would be. Five seemed like a lot. If someone has five houses, I generally think, "Woah, this guy has a lot of houses".'

'We should have printed thousands.'

'I didn't have enough paper.'

'For thousands?'

'No, for any more than five.'

'You only had five sheets of paper?'

'Three actually. That one under the windshield is printed on the back of an electricity bill. The one I've lost was printed on a phone bill.'

'This isn't going to work then, is it?'

'Keep the faith,' I said.

Just then, a strong gust of wind blew the poster off the side of the pub. It ran out into the middle of the road, across towards a roundabout, and then out of view entirely. The poster, not the pub. The pub didn't move. Pubs don't.

No-one used the phone box for the half-an-hour Anna and I sat and watched it. The poster tucked under the car windshield wipers blew away too. Well, it blew away after the man who owned the car came back, ripped it from his windshield, scowled at it like it had punched his wife (or girlfriend or boyfriend or dog, I didn't get to know him that well so I don't know his home situation), then balled it up and threw it towards a bin. It missed the bin, then blew away. All of which meant that we had one poster left. Anna fetched it back.

'I think you should just hold it,' she said. 'Let's just walk around and you can hold it up.'

'Or we could tape it to my face? I could walk around with it over my face?' I said.

'But you look mental.'

'I haven't done it yet. This is just my face.'

'I know.'

'Come on,' I said, attempting to rally the troops. Troop. Attempting to rally the *troop*. 'We can still do this! The poster campaign …'

'Campaign?'

'Bit strong?'

'That Volkswagen "Lemon" ad was a campaign,' said Anna. 'This is …'

'A joke, a folly, a waste of time? The Scottish Premier League, basically?'

'Stop it Adam. Stop making that joke.'

'Sorry. But fine, even though the poster idea was a wash-out, I used to be a journalist. I know how to find people. We will not leave Orpington tonight without having met Scott Minto.'

'We probably will leave Orpington tonight without having met Scott Minto.'

'Come on Anna. Be positive.'

'OK, we *definitely* will leave Orpington tonight without having met Scott Minto.'

* * * * *

For the next few hours, we roamed around pubs and coffee shops and supermarkets, asking staff and customers and total strangers if they knew who Scott Minto was, and if they knew where he lived. Most of the time I asked, this happened:

FADE IN.

EXT. STREET SCENE

ADAM is standing in the middle of a quite busy pavement. To his left is a row of small shops – a bakery, a coffee shop, a slightly nicer coffee shop. He is a quite short man in his mid-to-late 20s, more confident in himself than he ought to be, and sports what he would call a beard but other people might call 'fluff'. He is holding a poster with a man's face on it. A WOMAN is approaching. She is in her mid-30s and smartly dressed.

ADAM
Hello there, can you help me? I'm …

WOMAN
(shaking her head)
Sorry.

FADE OUT.

And it was a literally identical scene for poor old Anna. She too experienced a great deal of hurtful shunning from the general public.

FADE IN.

EXT. STREET SCENE

ANNA is standing in the middle of a quite busy pavement. To her left is a row of small shops – a bakery, a coffee shop, a slightly nicer coffee shop. She is a very attractive woman in her late 20s[31]. She has the sort of welcoming face that people respond very well to. She is intelligent and wonderful and quite frankly, could do a lot better than a bizarrely self-assured, quite short man with a fluffy face. She is holding a poster with a man's face on it. A WOMAN is approaching. She is in her mid-30s and smartly dressed.

ANNA
Hello there, can you help me? I'm trying to find this man.

WOMAN
Oh. Is he lost?

• • • • • • •
31 Actually 30, but don't let her know I've told you.

ANNA
No, no. He's a footballer. I'm a big fan.

WOMAN
Sorry, no, I don't know him. Have you tried asking in the pubs around here?

ANNA
Not yet, but that's a good idea.

WOMAN
Sorry I couldn't be more help. Do you know that guy? He's staring at you.

ANNA
That's my boyfriend.

WOMAN
(pulls a face)
Oh.

FADE OUT.

We persevered for a couple of hours, until the poster of Scott began to get tatty and torn. Mainly because I kept folding it and tearing it. And then, inspiration struck. Or more accurately, I remembered something Anna and I had done once already, that might work this time. Or even more accurately, Anna suggested something quite clever to which I just nodded along dumbly.

We bought a postcard. And on that postcard (picture of a small horse, much better than the one we sent Philippe), I wrote Scott a little message. I explained who I was, and why I was writing to him. In the address section, I just wrote 'Scott Minto, Orpington'. And once I had finished, I showed it to Anna, who smiled. This, she said, would probably work. Orpington was a small place, and the postmen would probably recognise a name as unusual as 'Minto'.

I skipped gaily over to the nearest post box and with something of a flourish, slapped the postcard inside. Then I realised I hadn't put the stamp on and we went through the whole thing again. My flourish was smaller the second time around.

* * * * *

After a few more hours of fruitless wandering, Anna and I were beginning to lose hope. And after a few dozen bemused looks from members of staff in Orpington eateries and newsagents, I was beginning to think Anna was right about sticking Scott's poster on my face. It was causing more problems (one) than it was solving (none). As the poster began to separate into two equally shabby sections, I finally gave up, and threw it away.

Anna and I headed for a drink. It was a quiet drink, but then most drinks don't say much. Anna and I did most of the talking. Most of it was about Scott Minto. Some of it was overheard by someone else. That someone else got off his chair, got on his bike (legs), and came over.

'You talking about Scott Minto?' he said, his hot breath thudding into my face. He smelled like his entire DNA was made out of pints.

'Yep,' I replied. 'Do you know him?'

'Yeah. Played for Chelsea didn't he?'

'He did. But do you know him?'

'Like, as a person?'

'Yes.'

'Oh, nah.'

'OK, no worries then.'

'He played for Charlton as well.'

'Yes he did.'

'And a Spanish team, if that helps?'

'Benfica.'

'Nah, they're Portugal. He works on Sky now.'

'He presents their Spanish football coverage.'

'That's right. As I say, he played for a Spanish club.'

'*Benfica.*'

'Nah, they're Portugal. He works on Sky now though …'

I stopped there, before the whole thing turned into something from a Bill Murray film. Throughout this little exchange, Anna had been busying herself with her mobile. She seemed happy enough to let me deal with the very drunk man. As he tottered off, his clothes flapping around him like a shoal of fish trying and failing to stay in close formation, Anna slid her phone under my nose.

'It's Scott's address,' she said. 'Well, his road anyway. I don't have a house number.'

'How did you find it?'

'It was quite easy, actually. But I feel a bit weird telling you, because now that you're writing a book about all this, then you'll have to include it in there, and that feels like an invasion of privacy. I don't think you should tell people how to find someone else's address.'

'I think you're right. Scott is probably a really nice dude. I don't want to upset him.'

'Exactly.'

'Maybe if I *don't* explain how you found it, it'll add an element of mystery to proceedings. And people love mystery. Look at Harry Potter. Look at other books whose name I don't know which probably also include mystery at the heart of their appeal.'

'Like Sherlock Holmes.'

'Yes, exactly.'

'Although Arthur Conan Doyle normally explained how Sherlock did things,' said Anna. 'That was part of his whole shtick. He would work something out, worm out some clue, then he would explain it.'

'But my book won't be as good as a Sherlock Holmes book, so I think we're alright just leaving it unexplained. It's nothing illegal though, is it?'

'Of course not. It's publicly-available information.'

'Phew.'

'So, shall we go to his house then?'

'No.'

'No?'

'Sorry, I meant yes. Yes. Let's go.'

And so off we went. We traipsed up hill and down dale, though mainly we just drove on some roads. As the evening began to set in, so the day got darker and began to turn into night. Experience had told me that normally happened once the sun went down, so I was prepared. I took off my sunglasses and turned my lights on (the car's lights). I felt like I was at the top of my game, organisation-wise.

After a few miles, we arrived at our destination. We looked at the beautiful houses on Scott's road. We looked for clues as to which one might belong to him – maybe he had painted it in Chelsea blue, Benfica red, or whatever colour Rotherham's away kit was when he played for them, grey maybe? – but alas, he had done none of those things. He hadn't even erected a Hollywood-style sign spelling out his own name. Truly, he was a footballer from a different era.

Anna suggested I go door-to-door, just knocking and hoping for the best. There was, she said, no other alternative. We were here. I had my camera and my sticker album with me. The only other thing I needed was some good luck.

'Good luck!' shouted Anna.

With her well wishes ringing in my ears, I set off towards house number one.

A few minutes later, I turned around and got back into the car.

'I can't do this,' I said.

'Why not?' replied Anna.

'Because this feels weird.'

'How is it weird?'

If this was a film, the camera would have cut to a very wide shot of my tiny little car, lit from the inside by the weak bulb of the overhead light, stranded on a completely quiet road, in the near total darkness.

'It's too late. It's dark. I can't knock on his door at this time of the day, he'll think I'm a weirdo. How would you feel if a man knocked on your door at this time of the evening, in the darkness, and asked you if he could take a picture of you for his sticker album?'

'I'd ask him who he thought I played for.'

'Be serious.'

'You're right. This isn't the right way to do this. Even if he answers the door, he'll never agree to meet with you ever again. You'll never get his photo for the book.'

I turned the in-car light off, and started the engine. An animal – furry, four-legged, ginger in colour, about two feet long, with a tail and pointy ears and reflective eyes like those 'cat's eyes' you see on the motorway – ran in front of the car. I asked Anna what it was, but she said she didn't see it, so I've included the description in the hope someone can identify it. We pulled out of Scott's road, and started the journey back to Southsea.

* * * * *

The following morning:

'What do you mean "it's not here?" Calm down, Adam. It has to be here somewhere.'

'It's missing! It's [*bleep*]ing missing!'

'Calm down. We'll find it. By the way, another letter arrived for you. I opened it. It's another sticker of Peter Atherton.'

'I don't care! I just need to find the sticker album!'

'OK. Let's start with the car.'

Ten minutes later:

'OK, it's not in the car. But at least we found this …'

'I don't need a poster of Scott Minto's face right now, Anna. I need my sticker album!'

'Relax. We'll find it. Let's retrace our steps. Maybe you left it in the service station. Let's go.'

Fifty minutes later:

'A *what*, sir?'

'A sticker album. A football sticker album.'

'I'm sorry sir, but we've not had a sticker album handed in.'

'Can you *please* double-check. It's a Merlin *Premier League 96* album.'

'96?'

'That's right.'

'When did you leave it here?!'

'Yesterday.'

'Yesterday, OK.'

'Yes. What, you think I left it here in October 1995 and I'm only now coming back to look for it? I left it here yesterday!'

Fifteen minutes later:

'If it's not in the car …'

'Which it isn't.'

'… and it's not at the service station …'

'Which it also isn't.'

'… then there is only one place it could be: the place where you can last remember having it in your hands. Orpington.'

'Orpington! Of course. So what are we going to do?' I asked.

'We'll just have to turn around and head back there, right now,' said Anna, in an act of outrageous kind-heartedness. 'And we'll just have to hope that Scott Minto hasn't been for a late-night or early-morning stroll and found it.'

'Why?'

'Because if he finds it, he's obviously going to check for his own photo – how could he not? – and then he's going to find that it's not there. And that will probably freak him out.'

'Good point. And we'll just have to hope whatever that strange beast was that I saw hasn't chewed it's way through it.'

'It was a cat, Adam. A *cat*.'

'You didn't see it. It was something weirder than a cat: furry …'

'Cat.'

'… four-legged …'

'Cat.'

'… ginger in colour, about two feet long …'

'Cat.'

'… with a tail, and pointy ears …'

'Cat.'

'… and reflective eyes like those "cat's eyes" you see on the motorway.'

'It was a cat. Those motorway cat's eyes are named "cat's eyes" because they look like the eyes of a cat.'

'Oh.'

'*Oh*? Seriously, Adam?'

'I thought it was just a brand name.'

* * * * *

The realisation hit me, and hit me hard. Not about the 'cat's eyes' thing, but about my sticker album being missing. Imagine a really hard punch. Imagine an even harder one. It was much harder than that. If this particular realisation had been a boxer it would have been Mike Tyson. In fact, it would have been a robot Mike Tyson who had been designed to punch even harder than the real Mike Tyson punches. Actually, it would have maybe even been a second, even bigger robot Mike Tyson, designed to stop the first robot Mike Tyson by punching even harder than he could punch. You get the point. When I realised the album was gone, I felt as though I had been punched really hard. Mainly in the feelings.

The drive up to the service station near Guildford was terrible. The drive onwards up to Orpington after leaving the services empty-handed was even worse. Anna and I barely said a word to each other. Of course, because Anna is a wonderful and beautiful person, she periodically assured me that we *would* find the album.

But I didn't believe her. In my mind, the album was long gone – either battered to death and swept away by the weather, or mauled by the strange animal (maybe a 'cat') we had seen the previous evening.

This time around, passing through Pratts Bottom was an uncomfortable experience. I was going to say it was a 'crappy' experience, but I decided against it. I could also tell you that what I just did – namely, mentioning something, but pretending not to mention it – is called a paralepsis. I *could* tell you that. But I won't.

As we pulled into Scott's road, Anna and I began to scan the sides of the road for signs of something shiny. But there was nothing. We parked up and began to paw through the long grass for the album.

My phone vibrated in my pocket. An e-mail had arrived in my inbox. I opened it.

TO: Me
FROM: Annemette Lund @ Lyngby Boldklub
Subject: Lars Bohinen
Hi, Adam
    You could try this number 004xxxxxxxxx.
    B rgds
    Annemette Lund, Lyngby Boldklub

Months and months after I had sent speculative e-mails to Lars's former clubs, one had finally responded. But truthfully, I didn't feel all that great about it. Lars's telephone number was no good to me while my album was missing. A minute later, my phone vibrated again.

TO: Me
FROM: Joe Questier @ Derby County Football Club
Subject: Lars Bohinen
Hi Adam,
   Contact number for Lars pasted below.
   004xxxxxxxxx
   Thanks,
   Joe Questier

Anna and I searched through the bushes and shrubs for a few more minutes, until our jumpers were covered in mud and leaves, and every inch of greenery had been kicked and wrestled in the hope of finding my re-lost treasure. But there was nothing.

Anna continued to look, hacking ever deeper into the undergrowth and ever further from view, but I sat in the car, and pathetically, I had a little cry. It felt like the end of an adventure. *Premier League 96* was gone.

I had another little cry when I realised the book I was now officially writing would probably have a quite premature and disappointing ending. And then, as I normally did in situations like this, I sent an e-mail.

To: FIFA
From: Me
Hi FIFA, Adam again.
   This time I've lost my sticker album. It's really hard to pin this one on you, Count Blatter, but I just have a hunch that this is still your fault, somehow or other.
   As usual, I have enclosed a list of expenses to be paid. You will notice that, alongside the normal stuff like petrol and food, I have included '1 x lost sticker album'. I have conservatively valued the album at ten million pounds, but I will accept nine, because I know FIFA has World Cups and things to pay for.

As usual, I will accept payment by cheque, BACS transfer or in the form of a signed photograph of you, Count Blatter, shirtless and riding a pony.

Cheers,

Adam

P.S. Any news on the Cup Winners' Cup? I hope you're making progress. But if that progress involves the idea of 'group stages', then YOU ARE DOING IT WRONG.

Jokes, 28–30.

Dino Zoff. He never stays long.

'John, Collins; Collins, John' – A Dutch striker being introduced to a Scottish midfielder.

'The Germans are really on the back foot against the Russians here.'

(Football commentary/football commentator [Allied] commentating on the Battle of Kursk)

Fifteen

A FEW MORE minutes passed. I spent the time trying to work out what the hell I was going to do if the album really *was* gone. I decided I would just subtly increase the font size of the chapters in the first half of the book and hope the publishers wouldn't notice, then tack on a hurried ending where I decide I actually *didn't* care about the album in the first place, and that losing it in Scott Minto's street was somehow symbolic of how football has changed and all part of the carefully-weaved narrative. Or something. My phone vibrated again. Another message.

> TO: Me
> From: Richard #2
> Here you go Adam - Philippe Albert - 00 3xxxxxxxxxx

This was getting ridiculous. This moment should have been one of overwhelming joy. At long last, I finally had the number I had most wanted to get my hands on. And it was, as far as mobile numbers go, a thing of staggering beauty. It was simple and elegant and ruthlessly functional all at once, like a piece of brutalist architecture or Bastian Schweinsteiger.

But if I didn't find my album, I had no reason whatsoever to dial it. If I was Canadian, female, an ex-girlfriend of Ryan Reynolds and unaware of the meaning of the word 'ironic', I might have said it was ironic. But it wasn't ironic. It was just annoying.

While I was bashing my head against the dashboard in frustration, Anna – the lovely and brilliant Anna – had wandered off, so far off in fact, that she had become just a little brown-haired speck in the distance.

But then, quite suddenly, I noticed she was now a slightly bigger brown-haired speck. And a few seconds later, I noticed she was an *even* bigger speck. And as if by magic, in another few seconds' time she was a bigger speck still. She was either getting closer to me, or growing very quickly. After some quick calculations on a scrap piece of paper – which were rudely interrupted by Anna shouting at me and waving her hands above her head like this \O/ – I realised she must be running towards me.

And she was holding something, too. Poetically speaking, it was my immediate hopes and dreams. Literally speaking, it was a worthless hunk of junk. I'd long since stopped being able to tell the difference. Anna burst in through the passenger door, and handed me my album. I wiped the mud off Nicky Barmby's face, left the mud on Jamie Redknapp and David Ginola's out of petty jealousy, and clasped my old friend to my chest.

'It was in a bush, down there,' said Anna, pointing into the distance, her face glowing with happiness and sweat. Mainly happiness. She told me she had a theory on how my sticker album had ended up in a bush miles (yards) away from where we had parked up the previous evening.

'I think you put it on top of the car when you came back from not knocking on Scott's door last night. I think we then drove off and then, due to a combination of science and probably wind, it flew off the roof when we picked up a bit of speed.'

'Sweet theory.'

'Thanks. I've checked the album, and it looks like everything is in one piece. No pages are missing, it's not been ripped or torn or anything. One page does look a tiny bit grotty though ...'

Anna took the album from me, and turned to the Manchester United page. 'See here, this guy – Brian McClair – he looks a bit gross.'

'Don't worry about that. A French bird did that to him. Took a crap right on his face.'

Anna looked a bit confused.

'By "a French bird", I mean a seagull who lives in France,' I added. 'It wasn't Charlotte Gainsborough or the one from *Amélie* or anything.'

'Anyway, we're here, you've got the album back – shall we see which one of these houses belongs to Scott Minto?'

I shook my head. A leaf fell from my fringe, and down on to my lap. My jumper was covered in foliage. I looked and smelt like a homeless man. Scott might have been watching our frantic rummaging from his kitchen window, his finger poised to press 'call' on his landline and dispatch the police to come and remove us. This wasn't, I quickly realised, the right time to meet him. Another leaf fell from my hair, tickled its way down my cheek, and fluttered into the footwell.

We started the drive back to Southsea, but after a few hundred yards, Anna demanded that I stop. So I did. She reached back behind her seat, grabbed a sheet of paper and some sticky tape and jumped out of the car. I watched as she sprinted over to a telegraph pole and neatly attached an A4-sized poster of Scott Minto's face to it.

'He might see it on his way to work,' she said, once she had clambered back into the car. 'And think about it – if you were driving to work, and you saw a photo of your own face with a strange mobile number written beneath it, what would you do?'

'Dial the number, probably,' I said, before thinking (but not saying) that I would also probably call the five-o in a state of extreme fear for my safety.

'Exactly. All you need to do is wait for him to see it, and call you.'

Anna and I high-fived, and I started the engine. A gentle gust of wind whipped the poster from the pole and sent it flying into the distance.

Anna brushed this latest setback aside, and suggested hiring a plane and doing some skywriting over Scott's house. Or hiring a plane to drag a banner through the sky over his house. Or hiring a plane and a megaphone and flying over his house and just shouting at him for a bit.

'Your plans are way too air-based,' I said. 'Who are you, David Gower?'

'Is that a football joke?' she asked.

'Cricket.'

'Even worse,' she said.

Even if her latest ideas didn't quite hit the target, Anna still filled me with confidence. She told me that some day – by hook or by crook, come hell or high water, and by a third idiom I can't remember now, but which I think had something to do with wool

– I would meet Scott, and I would take his picture for my sticker album. As we trundled our way back to the south coast, she fell asleep. Her encouraging words rang in my ear, like an enormous bell or a thousand telephones. I believed her.

* * * * *

The following day, a Monday, passed in a flurry of work and e-mails and phone calls. One of the phone calls was from Anna, telling me she had looked into the cost of skywriting.

'I've looked into the cost of skywriting,' she said.

'Oh yeah? How much?'

'A lot. An *awful* lot of pounds.'

'I don't have an awful lot of pounds.'

'No. Plus, they generally only write about four or five words as a maximum. They told me that writing "Scott Minto, my name is Adam and I am a journalist writing a book about trying to complete my childhood sticker album, please contact me on 07xxxxxxxx" was impossible. The first words would have faded by the time they finished the last ones. Plus the pilot says he is rubbish at numbers. His "7s" end up looking like "1s".'

'Typical.'

'So, after collecting all that data, I have a recommendation for you.'

'Excellent. What is it?'

'I would recommend you seriously consider not doing any of that.'

I thanked her for the advice, and told her I would think about it.

Scott had obviously not received my postcard, read the e-mail Richard #1 had forwarded him, nor seen one of my posters, as he hadn't yet called. I did, however, have one unusual call from a withheld number. Someone shouted 'Scott Minto!' at me a few times. One of the posters had obviously been found by someone, but unfortunately, it had been found by a man who, judging by his phone manner, had a bicep where he should have had a head.

Now, I don't want to say he was an idiot – sorry, mistyped – I *do* want to say he was an idiot. He was an idiot. If I had the money I would have hired a skywriter to announce it, but we've already established that isn't a viable option.

I called Lars three times. The first time, he didn't answer. The second time, he didn't answer. The third time, he didn't answer either, which I thought was a little uncreative and predictable of him. Especially when you consider what a creative midfielder he was.

I called Philippe three times too. The first time, he didn't answer either. The second time, he didn't answer. The third time, he didn't answer. But in his defence, that's chiefly because he actually *did* answer the second time I called. And amazingly, the phone call actually went very, *very* well.

As I've already mentioned, the first one went unanswered, and the third call never happened. Are you following me? I've been writing for too long without a break and I think I might be rambling a little bit. I do hope I'm still being clear.

'Hello?' a deep, rich French-sounding man's voice cut off the familiar sound of the European dial tone mid-*boooooooop*[32].

'Hello, is that Philippe?' I said.

'Yes,' he replied.

I felt my heart begin to pound with adrenaline. I felt my blood begin to pound around my veins because my heart had begun to pound with adrenaline. I felt my temperature rise and felt little beads of sweat form on my brow because my blood was pounding around my veins because my heart had begun to pound with adrenaline. I swallowed hard, tried not to think too much about the fact I was speaking to the *actual bloody Philippe Albert*, and launched into a now familiar pitch. All the pounding and rising and sweating continued apace.

'Hi there Philippe, my name is Adam Carroll-Smith. I'm a football journalist in England and I'm writing a book about an old football sticker album of mine. Basically, there are six players missing, and I am trying to track down and meet them all and finally complete my album. So far I have met three of them: Gary Penrice, Stuart Ripley and Keith Curle, and I still have to meet Lars Bohinen, Scott Minto and, hopefully, yourself. It's hopefully going to be a book about obstession *(sp)*[33] and adventure and football and …'

• • • • • •

32 Seventeen.

33 A nervous slip of the tongue, often easily done in pressurised moments. Like the time when, during a job interview, I accidentally said the phrase 'absolutely fuck all' when I meant to say 'four years of superb education and experience, during which time I honed my ability to work in a team and on my own.'

'OK.'

'OK, well, I need to – if at all possible – meet you face-to-face, because I need to take your photo because – again, if this is at all possible – then I can make a sticker and stick it in my sticker album. Is that alright?'

'Yeah, sure.'

It was becoming clear that Philippe was not a big talker. A quick tally of our conversation so far reveals that while I had said 138 words, Philippe had said four. That is a 34.5 words to one ratio. And when you are dominating a conversation as much as I was, you begin to panic.

Or at least I do. I begin to feel as though I am not holding the other person's attention. I begin to worry that they are secretly stood opposite a friend of theirs, pointing at their phone and then doing the mime for 'crazy person' (circular motion with index finger next to the side of the head, specifically the temple area). And when I feel like that, I say things I don't mean. Like this.

'I'm in Belgium this coming week actually, are you free to meet? You're in Wanfercée-Baulet, right? I'm heading to Brussels, but I can come to you.'

I was absolutely *not* planning on going to Belgium. At least I wasn't until the words were coming out of my mouth.

'I *am* in Belgium this week, but only until Friday. Then I am off to Euro 2012. I won't be back until after the tournament.'

'OK, that's no problem. Maybe we should wait until you're back from Poland and the Ukraine? I can give you a call after the tournament, and then we can sort out the specifics? Is that alright?'

'OK.'

'Then it's a date!'

I punched myself hard, mainly in the face, for saying the phrase 'then it's a date!' to Philippe Albert, and only once I had done that and stopped crying did I end the call and allow myself a loud and prolonged cheer.

I tallied up the respective word counts from the conversation. I was at a whopping 204 words – and it would have been a neat, even 200 if I hadn't said 'then it's a date!' – while Philippe had said a paltry 30. Clearly, he was a man of few words. But that didn't matter, just so long as some of those few words included a big, fat, juicy 'yes' when I asked him to pose for a photo for my album, and an equally plump 'yes' when I asked him to smile in it.

I called Anna and told her the good news. She was thrilled to hear I had spoken to Philippe Albert, but appalled I hadn't asked about his moustache. She evidently hadn't forgotten about 'votre moustache est très impressionnant, puis-je brosser?' even if I had, temporarily.

But regardless of whether or not Philippe still had a moustache (almost certainly not), and whether or not I would ask to brush it (almost certainly not), the fact remained that this (almost certainly) *was* a huge breakthrough.

After all the ~~cyber-stalking~~ internet research, the unanswered phone calls and door-knocks and unreturned and possibly undelivered postcards, I had finally spoken to the man himself. And even better, he had told me he was happy (or at least, prepared) to meet me.

Sure, I might have to wait a month until the big day, but waiting was no big deal. After all, 'waiting' is just laziness with an end goal. It's focused procrastination. I could go on, but I won't (idleness with an aim).

And anyway, as Anna had rightly told me outside Scott Minto's (probable) house, I could afford to be patient, because there *was* no rush to complete the album, I just had to complete it, by hook or by crook, come hell or high water, as sure as wool is wool.

I remembered it was a Monday and, theoretically at least, I was supposed to be working, so I checked my e-mails. I had loads (four). They were all from Rosh. The first one was a normal sort of e-mail, asking me about the progress of some piece of work or other. The second was an e-mail asking why I hadn't replied to the first e-mail. The third was an e-mail asking why I hadn't replied to the first two e-mails. The fourth one, written all in caps, demanded I call him immediately. There were no exclamation marks. All caps plus no exclamation marks probably equalled trouble. Uh oh, I thought to myself.

I picked up my phone and dialled. I was positive that Rosh was about to shout at me. After the fifth ring, he answered.

He *was* angry. But it wasn't because of anything I had done. It was because of something Ed had done, which Rosh believed was somehow my doing. Ed had been placing bids on eBay for bulk lots of old Merlin football stickers. That morning, package upon package had arrived at the office. Unbeknownst to Rosh, Ed had spent the morning turning his desk into a mess of old and useless stickers and strips of torn cardboard. In a <idiom/>New York minute</idiom>, his productivity had <metaphor>dropped off a cliff</metaphor>, and he had become <simile>as aimless as a Danny Guthrie through ball</simile>.

Rosh huffed and puffed and complained that I had somehow spread my dumb sticker book obsession to another member of staff. I apologised and Rosh calmed down. Then I asked him to put me through to Ed so I could quiz him on how many of the stickers he needed he had found, and he put the phone down on me. I called Ed direct instead.

'So?' I asked, not bothering to say hello or introduce myself. 'How many stickers have you found?'

'Nine!'

'So how many do you still need?'

'Eight. And I've got two more packages arriving tomorrow. I reckon I could complete the album in less than a week!'

'What?!'

'I said I reckon I'm going to complete the album in a few days.'

'Yeah I know, I heard you. I meant "what?!" like "what the heck!"'

'Oh right.'

'But hold on: if you're going to complete your album in the next few days, that means you'll complete yours before I complete mine!'

'I guess so. How are you getting on, anyway? Any luck with Lars? Scott? Philippe?'

If I had been on a landline, I would have slammed the phone down. But as I was on my mobile, all I could do was press 'end call' a bit angrily, so I didn't bother. But my anger was very real. Realer than real. Really real. I was absolutely furious. Ed was going to complete his sticker album before me.

It shouldn't have mattered, but it definitely did. If I was making a list of 'trivial things that shouldn't be important to me but definitely are', it would have been right up there, somewhere near the top. Some long-dormant competitive sticker album instinct kicked back in. I didn't just want to complete the album, I wanted to do it before Ed.

'Ad? Adam?'

'Sorry,' I said, even though I wasn't sorry about anything. 'What were you saying?'

'I asked how you were getting on with Lars Bohinen. Any luck?'

'Not really.'

'Scott Minto?'

'Not really.'

'Philippe Albert?'

'He's in the bag.'

'Oh well. Hold on, *what*?!'

'I've got his mobile number. I've spoken to him. I asked him if I could come over and visit him. And he said *yes*.'

'Shit!'

'Don't swear. I'm trying to keep the book swear-free.'

'Can't you bleep it out?'

'I have been so far, but I can't be bothered anymore. Just don't swear.'

'OK. But anyway, that's amazing about Philippe! Fuck. Shit. When are you going to see him? Bollocks. Fuck.'

If Ed hadn't found nine of the 17 he had needed, if he hadn't mentioned the fact he was *still* holding one of the stickers I still needed, and if he hadn't bragged about being closer to completing his re-discovered collection than I was to finishing *my* album and then sworn four times in one sentence, then I might not have said what I said next.

I might have stuck to the original plan. But I didn't. I didn't tell Ed I was going to see Philippe Albert in Belgium once he had got back from commentating at Euro 2012. I told him I was leaving tomorrow.

'I'm leaving tomorrow,' I said. 'Bang!'[34]

· · · · · · ·

34 'Try to end your chapters with a bang.' (*p.1000, Book Writing for Idiots, Costanza Publishing, 2012*)

Art, 6.

ICH WÜRDE
VIELMEHR GERADE
DIE BUNDESLIGA.

FOOTBALL HIPSTER BADGE.
(CUT OUT AND KEEP)

Sixteen

AT ABOUT 6.30am, I called Rosh and told him I needed the day off. He must have been in a good mood or still asleep because he agreed almost immediately, which was just as well. I was calling from Dover ferry port.

This time around, the journey to Europe was less eventful. There was no Frenchman on the ferry. There were some French men, but no French*man*. No sea birds defecated on any of my treasured childhood possessions either. I did, however, keep an eye out for the bird that had done something like that the last time I was on this ferry. Unfortunately for me – and this might be racist – all seagulls look the same to me.

I made my way through France and onwards towards Belgium with the utmost (100 out of 100) ease. I drove on the right of literally every single most of the roads. I crossed the border into Albert country at lunch (the time, not the meal), and ate the sandwiches Anna had lovingly prepared for me, and once I had finished, chewed the chewing gum she had also packed, so my breath would smell nice when I met Philippe.

It was the latest in a string of ridiculously kind gestures she had made towards me, each of which convinced me a little more that maybe, hopefully, she felt the same way about me as I felt about her. As I ate the final mouthful of my chicken, mozzarella and pesto sandwich, I felt like a muppet (Gonzo) that I was still too much of a coward to (or Beaker) tell her I was in (no, Fozzy) love with her (Rizzo).

I called Philippe on my hands-free and his mobile rang through to voice-mail. I thought about leaving him a message, then thought against it. For a while, the two thoughts scrapped it out. I left the pair of them to it and concentrated on driving. 'Don't leave a message' won on points, so I ended the call.

I pressed on, along the empty Belgian motorways, until Homer Simpson – my sat-nav was back on board – steered me on to the quieter, more rural final roads which led to Wanfercée-Baulet. As I drove down the sort of familiar residential streets towards Philippe's house, I was surprised by how at home I felt. Namely, *very*. Which was surprising, as I didn't, don't and probably never will live there.

I parked up on Philippe's road, got out, and knocked on the front door. Still nothing. I rang the house phone. No answer. I rang Philippe's mobile. He answered and told me he was right nearby and would meet me in two minutes. In opposite land, he did that. In reality, he didn't pick up.

I eased open the letterbox and shouted 'hellooooooo!' through it. The house was quiet and empty. I decided, in what was quite a weird move, to do a little controlled experiment. I took my chewing gum out of my mouth, and stuck it in the middle of the front door. That way, I reasoned, I could just drive past every so often, and check to see if the gum was still there. If it was, that meant no-one was home. But if it was gone, that meant someone was in.

I got back in my car and decided to go for a little drive; to gather my thoughts, practise what I was going to say when I met Philippe, and to quietly ask myself why I had just done that completely mental thing with the chewing gum.

As I drove aimlessly around the Belgian countryside, I noticed a few things. First, that Belgium was ridiculously flat. Second, that my car smelt like old cheese. And third, that there, away in the distance, was a rickety football stand jutting out above all the flatness. I headed towards it in the hope it would get nearer. Thanks to logic and maths, it did.

I parked up on a dusty little patch of land beside the tatty little ground. I took a quick look around and found a battered sign on a rusty gate, which had 'RJS' written on it. A brief Google later, I discovered this was the home of RJS Heppignies Lambusart-Fleurus, a team in the lower reaches of the Belgian league system, but the upper reaches of the 'teams with long names' league.

I felt peculiarly excited to be there. This was a real football ground. The grass was overgrown, the goals looked wonky. Behind the one closest to me, a small, single-storey clubhouse stood, tired, its paintwork faded and peeling. It was a world away from the sort of football stadiums I had, metaphorically and geographically, left behind in England. I felt an overwhelming urge to climb over the little fence and have a kickabout.

But I had more important things to do. I went back to my car, started the engine and turned my sat-nav back on. Before I pulled away and back to Philippe's house, I checked my e-mails on my phone. I had two new messages from Ed. The first one was an amended list of the eight stickers he still needed to complete *Premier League 96*. The second, sent about ten minutes later, was three words long, 'Make that seven'.

As I stared at my phone and began formulating an only half-pretend plan to break into Ed's house and steal that Lars Bohinen sticker, a horrible, chilling feeling swept through me, as though a looming and malevolent presence was nearby. 'Turn around!' yelled Homer. 'Turn around!'

I lifted my eyes from my mobile screen and turned my head slowly to my right. And then I screamed. I screamed a scream like one of the kids in the film *Scream*, or one of the slightly older kids in *Scream 2*. Stood next to me, his face pressed more-or-less (mainly more) right up against the driver-side window, was a small, wide-eyed and quite (very) fat Belgian man.

'Turn around! Turn around!' screeched Homer once more.

I screamed again.

Once I had finished screaming, I theatrically patted my chest in what I thought was the international mime for 'you scared me, guy!' The little Belgian just stared at me dumbly. The thought crossed my mind that he might be one of the un-dead; that he could be a Belgian zombie on the lookout for human flesh. I asked him a couple of times, but he just shrugged. He was either a particularly un-hungry zombie, or he wasn't one of the un-dead.

I took my chances, and got out of the car. I coughed up a bit of conversational French, but unfortunately, the conversation I was having was mainly about the whereabouts of the town swimming pool. Which wasn't that helpful. This was a day-trip, after all. I hadn't even packed any trunks.

'What are you?' the Belgian asked, quite unexpectedly.

'Journalist. English. England,' I replied, over-selling myself.

'And why are you here?' he asked.

What an extremely philosophical, existential question for a small Belgian with dirty fingernails to ask, I thought to myself. I fell silent and contemplated the nature of human existence for a bit, then I saw a quite big dog on the other side of the road chewing itself and stopped. I decided to tell him, (the Belgian, not the dog) as succinctly as possible, in his mother tongue, why I was in his village.

'Je suis ici pour ...'

I tried to remember the verb for 'to see' or 'to meet'. Neither sprang, or even hopped, to mind. But like a snow-shoveller crossing a picket line, I ploughed on in spite of everything. I remembered the verb for 'to brush'. I went with that.

'Je suis ici pour brosser ...'

I stopped myself before I finished the sentence. I guessed that if I told this man I was here to brush Philippe Albert, he might call the mounties or Kim Clijsters or Dr Evil or whoever it is that actually enforces the law in Belgium. In the end, I did what I do whenever I struggle with the English language, and just gave up on verbs altogether. I got my album out of my bag and showed him the Newcastle page. I pointed to Philippe's empty space. 'Je suis ici pour Philippe Albert,' I said.

The little Belgian's face lit up. He jumped into the air, his heels kicking up two tiny clouds of dust, and powerfully headed an imaginary football into an imaginary goal, beyond the reach of an imaginary keeper. Or maybe he was making an imaginary defensive header to prevent an imaginary striker from scoring an imaginary goal. I don't know.

'Oui,' I said. 'Oui! Football!'

He broke into breakneck French, from which I managed to pluck the word 'voiture'. He pointed at my car, and I tentatively made my way back towards it. I got in, realised I had left the engine running this whole time, and waited for my next instructions from the little Belgian. He ran over, jumped in the passenger seat and proceeded to direct me back the three or so miles to Wanfercée-Baulet.

We drove on, past Philippe's road, until we reached a dusty, private road, which seemed to lead nowhere. He told me to stop, got out, then walked around to the front of the car. He stared at me for a few seconds, then began to walk backwards, waving his arms as though asking me to follow him. So I did. I crawled along at walking pace behind him – he eventually turned around, and every now and again, looked over his shoulder to make sure I was still following – as he led me along the dirt track, up through a narrow cross roads of residential streets, and finally into another, very picturesque private road.

Suddenly, he stopped walking, and I looked at where I was. I was somewhere near the 'h' in nowhere, surrounded by green fields, green trees and some admittedly very nice houses. I began to wonder what the flip was going on. Then I began to wonder why I hadn't begun to wonder what the flip was going on a little sooner.

The Belgian wandered back to the passenger-side window, leaned in, and said 'here, here', and pointed down the road. And then he walked back out in front of my car, and began his slow march once more. We turned a gentle corner, and as if by magic, a house appeared. Without turning around, the Belgian pointed, quite nonchalantly, at the house, then raised the thumb of his right hand into the air.

There was a neat electric gate at the entrance to the house's driveway. Beyond that, stood a beautiful red brick home. I heard the whinny of a horse. The Belgian walked back towards me, this time passing by the driver-side window. He stopped, and kicked an imaginary football. He pointed at the house.

'Philippe, yes?' he said. 'Philippe Albert.'

'This is his house?! *La maison de Philippe, oui*?!' I asked.

He nodded, turned around and walked off.

I walked up to the little gate. Beside it was a small electronic panel, on which there was an intercom button and a speaker. While I thought about pressing the button, I felt a gentle Belgian breeze blow my hair (mainly the bit at the front) across my forehead. I heard another horse whinny, or maybe the same horse whinnying again. I could just about hear Homer Simpson, a few feet behind me.

'Turn around!' he said. 'Turn around!'

* * * * *

176

When I was a kid, I thought I knew a lot about football. I thought I understood tactics at a more advanced level than my peers – I was always stood in space, holding my position like a beardless Pirlo, while everyone else just chased the ball – and I really thought I knew more about the players and the clubs than my school buddies. If you had asked me 100 times whether I knew just about everything there was to know about football, I would have said 'yes', 99 times. The other time, I would have said 'definitely yes'.

There was one kid at school who claimed to be as much of a football geek as me. His name was Tom. It was a pretty fitting name, because I always did want to hit him rhythmically over the head with a drumstick. We never swapped stickers, because we didn't want to help the other succeed. At that time, if you had asked me 100 times if he was my nemesis, I would have said 'yes', 99 times. The other time, I would have said 'who is Tim?' because sometimes I don't pay attention so well.

I prided myself on knowing more about football than Tom. So the first time I was forced to accept I wasn't quite the know-it-all I thought I was, the realisation hit me hard. Please refer to the previous metaphor I used about Mike Tyson and robots for a fuller understanding of what that felt like. But in a nutshell, it felt bad to be proved wrong.

To cut a long story short, I had been acting under the totally wrong assumption that when a player put one in his own net, it was called a 'home goal'. I knew that they were listed as an (o.g.) in the results section of *Shoot!* and *Match*, but I never, ever thought I might be wrong. I was a bit of a dick like that, I suppose.

One day, Tom picked me up on my error. I fought my corner, convinced I was right, despite the mounting mountain of evidence to the contrary. Only once half the boys in my year had called me a 'dinlo', did I back down.

I felt like an idiot. I made a silent promise to myself that if I was ever wrong about something else in the future, I would be more contrite. I would admit my error, and try to put it right. I apologised to Tom for being so stubborn, and for calling him a 'nob-head'. I gave him my Dip-Dab by way of reparations. He told me he would have preferred a Refresher bar, so I called him a 'nob-head' again, at which point I felt bad again, and bought him the Refresher bar. He didn't say thank you. I waited until he was out of sight before calling him a 'nob-head' again because I was running out of money.

Back in Wanfercée-Baulet, I was experiencing a similar feeling of guilt. If this was *the* Philippe Albert's house – and given that I had been led here by someone who appeared to know who he was, I had no reason to think it wasn't – then that meant only one thing. I had made a mistake. There were, unbelievably, two P. Alberts in Wanfercée-Baulet, and I had been knocking on the wrong one's door.

The one who had almost definitely *never* played for Newcastle. The one who *wasn't* in my sticker album. I had been annoying a random and probably very nice Belgian via postcard, telephone and unarranged home visits.

I looked at the little 'intercom' button on the electronic panel beside me, and decided Homer Simpson was right. I had to turn around. I had something more important do before I pressed this button.

And so I drove away from Philippe Albert's house, and back towards the other P. Albert's house. I stopped at the little shop nearby, the same one where I had bought Anna's postcard, and bought another. The same one, in fact, which featured some Belgian stones. I wrote six words on the back. 'Please ignore previous postcard. Apologies. Adam'.

I looked for a Dip-Dab too, but the shop didn't sell them. But as I walked to the front door to post the card, I remembered that I already had something much better than a bag of sherbet. I pulled the Belgian scratchcard from my wallet, and popped it, along with the postcard, as quietly as I could through the letterbox. I gently prised the chewing gum from the front door, and said a silent farewell to *a* Monsieur Albert. And then I drove off to meet *the* Monsieur Albert.

I called Philippe and this time, he picked up. I told him I was in Belgium, and free to see him today. He told me to pop round later in the afternoon. I drove back to the RJS football ground, and waited.

I called Anna and told her the good news. She reminded me that I was to open any conversation with our agreed French phrase. I managed to barter my way to only saying it if Philippe *actually* had a moustache. Anna reluctantly agreed. I crossed my fingers that when I saw Philippe, he would be clean shaven.

I called Ed too, chiefly to gloat about my impending meeting with Philippe Albert, but also to check up on his sticker book progress. He hadn't found any new stickers, but he did tell me he was considering growing a moustache, and asked if I could probe Philippe for any 'tache-growing tips. I told him I would, in return for his Lars Bohinen sticker. He told me to make like a pepper, and get stuffed. I told him to make like someone trying to send a large file by e-mail, and zip it. Which is a computer joke.

A couple of hours passed, during which time a combination of hunger, laziness, curiosity and mounting poverty led me to eating a mouthful of the dashboard toastie. And as I sat in the shadow of the raggedy stand, I also watched two tramps in TRON helmets having a sword fight, a high-speed blimp race, and Jean-Marc Bosman eating an entire birthday cake with someone else's name piped on to it, while laughing hysterically and shouting 'Bosman rules! Bosman *ruuuulllllllleeeeessssss!*'[35]

After all that excitement, I was worried my meeting with Philippe might fall flat. But as I pulled up to his home and saw the man himself, pottering about in his garage, all those concerns disappeared. The little electronic gate whirred open, and Philippe waved me through on to his driveway. I parked up and he strolled over to meet me. There was no moustache on his face, or anywhere else.

'Hi Adam,' he said, extending his hand. He was enormous – at a guess, well over 15 feet high – but his face had a calming, welcoming quality.

'Hi Philippe,' I said, shaking his hand which, at a guess, was the same size as my torso. 'Thanks so much for meeting with me.'

'No problem. Come on inside,' he said. So I did. I followed Philippe Albert into Philippe Albert's house, sat down at Philippe Albert's kitchen table where Philippe Albert offered me a drink and a biscuit and I thought about just how ridiculous and awesome this whole situation was. It couldn't, surely, get any better.

And then I tasted the biscuit.

It was the *best fucking biscuit I've ever eaten.*

• • • • • • •

35 Not true. I didn't see Jean-Marc Bosman. Everything else, though.

Choose your own adventure!

There are two versions of the following chapter – a clean version and an absolutely appalling, x-rated, horrifyingly explicit version.

To read the clean version, turn to page 181.
To read the explicit version, turn to page 188.

Good luck.

Seventeen

'If I was 20 years old now, I would not play football. I would do something else,' said Philippe.

'Seriously?! You wouldn't even want to be a pro?'

'No. You give me the chance to play now, I would say no. I loved my career, but I would do something different if I was a young player now.'

'Like what?' I asked.

'If I hadn't been a professional footballer, I would probably have ended up working in a factory in south Belgium. I would rather do that now, because I would not enjoy playing as much.'

I asked Philippe what he meant. He shrugged.

'I think teams have to win at all costs now, because managers know they could get sacked at any minute. A lot of the football in England now is very negative. I think I would get in trouble playing now, because even though I was a defender, I liked to play football. I liked to come out of defence with the ball, I liked to get forward and attack. I liked to express myself.

'I would probably get shouted at for doing that in the Premier League now. There is not so much room for individuals now. Tactically the Premier League has changed so much and the football is less entertaining. Most teams play with the same tactics – they try to cancel each other out.

'You only have to look at big games between the big teams now. Compared to fifteen years ago, these games are very boring and defensive, because they are games between two teams who want to avoid *losing* first, not try to win. But if you think of the famous Newcastle–Liverpool games, you had two teams playing to *win* the game.

'I understand that, of course, because if Manchester City try to win games and lose because they are being too attacking, then the manager knows he is going to be sacked very quickly. But that is not English football. English football *is* attacking football.

'That's why Kevin Keegan won't be back in football ever again; it's not his era now. It's the era of "safety first". English football is still fast and intense and competitive, but is it still attacking, with teams trying to win games? No, I don't think so. And it's the same almost everywhere. I wouldn't enjoy playing football like that.'

I couldn't quite believe what I was hearing. This was not bluster or posturing. He meant all of it. I was flabbergasted (or 'shocked', for the laymen), because in many ways, Kevin Keegan's 1995/96 Newcastle were one of the teams who most clearly defined my relationship with football in my formative years.

They were exciting, joyous, cavalier. In Keegan, they had a manager who fostered an almost paternal spirit of kinship and belonging among his team and their supporters. I secretly longed to be a Geordie throughout that 1995/96 season.

And in Philippe, every bit as much as Asprilla, Shearer or Ferdinand, Newcastle possessed a footballer who clearly defined Keegan's era in charge of the Magpies. Philippe was comfortable on the ball, eager to get forward, skilful. He seemed to play the game with such transparent joy and enthusiasm. His chip over Peter Schmeichel – a singularly delicious and hazy arc – made me re-think exactly what a defender could be. And now he was telling me he would rather work in a factory than be a modern-day Premier League footballer.

I already knew a lot had changed in football over the past couple of decades. I knew my relationship with the game had become more complicated and a little strained. And Stuart and Gary and Keith had all said the same things Philippe was saying to me now – that the game was less joyous, less entertaining, less *fun*. But to hear Philippe say it so starkly really hammered the point home. Joy and entertainment and fun were the things which made me fall in love with football. Those were the things I had been trying to reconnect with.

'And the money they make now,' Philippe shook his head, 'it would not make me happy. For some, it's more than three, four, five million pounds a year. Can you imagine that sort of money? I can't. When they earn that sort of money, footballers can't live in the same world as normal people, and I have always considered myself a normal person, due to my upbringing and my education. I have always wanted a normal life. I just want to be me.

'I feel lucky to have played when I did, because I feel that when I played, football was still a part of normal life; a part of the real world. In 1996, the best players were on £20,000 a week and that was really a lot of money, but now people earn £200,000 and that is out of order, it is a negative thing. Anyone would lose touch with the real world earning money like that. That sort of money makes you forget about the meaning of money.

'I read about players like Mario Balotelli, and how Manchester City are paying him unbelievable wages. I don't feel any jealousy about that – that is good for Balotelli – but I think about how, in the Manchester area, you have people who are very poor. You have people who, at the end of the month, don't have the money to feed their kids. You have people who work two or three jobs. There is a great inequality [in that].

'Of course, it is not the footballers' fault they earn this much money when other people don't, but I don't *understand* it. I would not be able to be happy earning so much money knowing that. That's not how I see life. I would rather live closer to the real world.

'That's why when I finished playing, I just wanted a normal living, a normal job. I just live a normal life with my family. Look around ...' he gestured to the walls of his living room and kitchen, '... there are maybe two pictures of me from my playing days, but my shirts are not here, because football was just my career. I did not play the game to be famous or anything like that – it was just a job, a very *good* job – but I was not a movie star, just a normal man.

'But now players have all that power, especially since Bosman. In the Premier League, they are all millionaires now. Now when they sign contracts, it is more about money, I think. Whenever I signed contracts it was never about that. Maybe that is because there was less money involved, but when I saw Keegan in Leeds before signing my contract with Newcastle, we talked money for two minutes. The rest of the time we talked about football. The most important thing for me was to know I was going to play and to play for a special team.

'That sort of joy is gone a bit for players I think, because of the money. Money has changed the mentality of players. They don't respect each other, the manager, or the fans. I remember after we beat United 5-0, Cantona, Scholes, Beckham, Giggs, Roy Keane – they all had a beer with the Newcastle players and we talked football. There was that joy to the game. It was the best era to be a player, because it was still the old mentality: we played hard, but we had a few beers with the opposition in the players' lounge afterwards. We were friendly and professional, and there was more respect – for your colleagues, chairman, your manager and the fans.

'To me, English football was the birthplace of the game, but money is even changing the traditions in England. I grew up as a Liverpool fan – the English game was popular even here in Belgium – so even as a foreigner, I had always wanted to play there. It was so full of history.

'I loved the traditions and the history of English football and [in particular] the oldest competition, the FA Cup. But now, clubs would rather finish fourth rather than win the FA Cup. *That* is what money has done. It has made finishing fourth better than winning such a historic trophy. That is very sad.

'And yeah, the best players want to play in England now and that is great, but there are too many foreigners. The identity of football in England used to be strong. There were many Irish, Scottish, Welsh and English players when I came over, but not anymore. That is not right, and it is affecting the national team, too.

'The Premier League is not good for England's national team. I think they will struggle to qualify for tournaments in the future because the Premier League is too powerful. But it is more important, it seems, that the Premier League is successful than England's national team. That is because of money.

'But you can also say money has changed international football. It used to be the highest level of the game. But because clubs have more power than national teams, because they pay the players and they don't want them injured, international football isn't as important anymore. It used to be a shop window, like for me at the World Cup in 1994, but players don't need it anymore. The Champions League is the highest level now, because it is the tournament with the most money.'

Philippe paused, and took a sip of water. He was a passionate and articulate man, and it made me feel pretty sad that he was seemingly so disillusioned with football. How could this have happened? Before I could ask, Philippe's wife returned home and crept through to the kitchen, her arms full with bags of shopping. Philippe told me we would have to wrap things up so he could help with the unpacking. I took the chance to ask him one more question.

'There's a lot wrong with the game, or at least it seems like there is,' I said. 'How much would change, right now, if you were in charge?'

'A lot.'

'But do you still *love* the game?'

'Of course,' he said, with a smile.

I got my camera out, and Philippe posed up. After a few clicks, the deed was done.

PHILIPPE ALBERT

At this point in proceedings, I got a little brave. I was about to leave – and leave with the all-important photo safely stored on my memory card – so I did something a little risky. I said something to Philippe in French. Yeah. That.

'Votre moustache était très impressionnant,' I said, conjugating être like a native.

He pretended not to hear me, and I pretended I hadn't said anything. I was pretty pleased I didn't open with it. The afternoon might not have gone so well.

* * * * *

I got back to Dover at 20 past crazy o'clock, Wednesday morning. At some sort of checkpoint in the dock, a man in a bright-yellow jacket whose face looked like a clenched fist with eyebrows asked me to stop. My car, not me in general. I rolled my window down (the car's window) as instructed, and he began to ask me some questions. Firstly, where I had been.

'Belgium,' I said.

His knuckly face didn't flinch. He asked me how long I had been out of the country.

'A day. One day. The day before now. Yesterday.'

He asked me what the purpose of my visit had been.

'Business,' I replied, but only because saying 'pleasure' would have sounded weird and probably invited more questions. His scary face seemed to want a more specific answer.

'I went to meet Philippe Albert, the former Newcastle centre-half. Centre-back. Defender. Footballer. Man. Human man,' I said, being as specific as I possibly could. Old fist-face looked confused, then waved me through. If you ever go through Dover port and get stopped, please use the same answers, just to confuse the man in the yellow vest.

I drove back to Southsea and headed straight to Anna's flat. I let myself in – she had given me a key by this point, I wasn't breaking and entering – and helped myself to a drink from her fridge. Away in the bedroom, Anna woke up. Probably because of all the cheering.

She called me into the bedroom, and as I sat on the edge of the bed taking my shoes off, Anna sat up, leaned over to her bedside table, then handed me an envelope with my name written on the front. I opened it and peered inside, just as I used to with every new packet of Premier League stickers. To my great surprise, there was a single sticker inside. From the back design, I could tell it was a *Premier League 96* sticker. I felt my heart race with excitement.

But the feeling didn't last long. The number, 332, was too high. Scott Minto's number was 280 and Lars Bohinen's was 15. I pulled the sticker out and turned it over. It was John Sheridan. I had no idea why, but it was definitely him. Before I could ask,

Anna explained why he was here. She said she had seen him on eBay. She bought the sticker, guessing it might come in useful. I thanked her for the gift, and kept my reservations about how useful it might be to myself.

'So how does it feel?' she asked.

'What?'

'How does it feel to have partied with Philippe Albert?'

'Partied is a bit strong. We drank tea.'

'Were there biscuits?'

'There were, actually.'

'Then it was a party,' she said, before flopping back on to her pillow and falling asleep.

* * * * *

With Euro 2012 kicking off in a few days' time and the Olympics following on after that, Ed and I decided to take the next eight weeks off from our respective sticker collecting quests. Not because we were competing in either you understand, but so we could both sit around and watch the football and the athletics and whatever sport Britain might be doing well in at that particular moment, safe in the knowledge the other wouldn't be off trying to complete his album.

At the agreement of this historic peace treaty that I-absolutely-did-not-plan-to-secretly-break-the-very-second-the-opportunity-arose-because-after-all-it-was-only-a-poxy-truce-made-over-the-phone-and-he-would-probably-do-the-same-given-the-chance, I double-checked that Ed didn't need a John Sheridan for his album. He did not.

He asked me if I thought this temporary suspension of sticker hostilities would hold. I told him if it didn't, it wouldn't be because of me.

Seventeen
[explicit version]

[REDACTED]

Eighteen

7 June 2012
Thursday

ACTUALLY, IT *would* be because of me. And it took less than a day. But it really wasn't my fault. I got an e-mail. This is what it said.

> Hi Adam,
>
>   A couple of people mentioned you were looking to talk to me. My number is 07xxxxxxxxx.
>
>   You can call me now if you want but will be off the phone from 2.30. Or we'll catch up soon.
>
>   Cheers,
>
>   Scott

I spent the next five (none) minutes (seconds) agonising (not agonising) over what (how long I should wait) to do (exactly what I wanted).

I genuinely thought about sticking to the terms of the peace accord. But then I genuinely did break it. I decided to feel proud of myself for lasting a full five (none) minutes (seconds) before giving in to temptation. I replied to Scott and told him I planned to call him later that afternoon. And then later that afternoon, I called him, just as I had planned. It was one of my better organised and executed plans.

For the first few minutes of our conversation, Scott appeared unsure about my motives. I don't want to put words in his mouth, but though he was a charming and polite man, I got the feeling he thought I was pretty weird. He didn't seem to get why I wanted to meet him and take his photograph. I think he might have worried

I was the sort of dude who had a secret 'Scott Minto' room in my house, a huge tattoo of his face on my stomach and who drank coffee from an Arielator.

That he might have thought any of that was my fault, because by this point, I had rattled off the same spiel about my sticker album so often that I had ceased to see that what I was saying was crazy.

I realised I would have to *really* explain why I wanted to meet Scott or he might never agree to meet me. So I re-doubled my efforts to persuade him I was sane. But then I realised that doubling 'no effort' still meant I was putting in 'no effort', and decided to 'up' my efforts instead.

That seemed to do the trick. Scott relented and agreed to meet me. He told me where he lived and I realised for the second time in succession that the address Anna had found for me was totally incorrect. Scott lived in a totally different village. I would have been angry, but by this point I was in love with her, so I decided not to say anything, or at least to save it until I did something wrong myself and I could throw it back into her face, as is the custom in Western relationships.

'So, we'll rendezvous a month tomorrow,' I said to Scott. 'You can fill me in on life at Sky Sports and I can explain the finer points of this sticker book thing I'm doing. The coffees will be on me. What's your flavour? I like vanilla lattes. Anyway, see you tomorrow Scott – I'm really looking forward to walking away with your picture for my album.'

I put the phone down, and felt a great sense of pride at setting a new personal best of getting four Craig David song titles into a single paragraph of speech.

Of course, even though my meeting with Scott was a few weeks away, agreeing to meet him before 12 August – the date when the ceasefire between Ed and I officially ended – still meant I would have to be sneaky. I couldn't ask Rosh for a day off during the week, because word would get back to Ed, and he might get suspicious.

This would have to be a stealth mission. But that was OK. I had a lot of experience of stealth missions. Sorry, mistyped. I had a lot of experience with sandwiches. But fortunately for me, Ed was a trusting man. And an easy one to confuse. I called him, and did my best to throw him off my scent. After two rings, he picked up.

'Hello, Ed speaking,' said Ed, accurately.

'Hi Ed, it's Adam here,' I added, introducing myself by name even though I knew Ed very well, because this was a telephone conversation and Ed did not have my face as a visual aid to establish who it was that was speaking to him. Given that I was about to deceive him, I thought it best to be as helpful as possible in the meantime.

'Hi mate. What's up?'

'Nothing much,' I lied. 'I'm just sitting at my desk, totally holding up my end of this truce and thinking about how I have no plans to break it until after the Olympics.'

'That's good to hear,' said Ed. 'That's good to hear,' he added, as if to emphasise how good it was to hear what I had just said.

'Yeah. I just thought I'd call to let you know.'

'Thanks, Adam. I feel reassured by that. I feel like I can truly trust you.'

'You *can* totally trust me. I'm a trustworthy guy. And I really mean that. Trust is more than a four-letter word to me.'

'It's a five-letter word.'

'Exactly. I don't want to over-egg the pudding here Ed, but I am *so* trustworthy. Did you know my middle *name* is actually Trust?'

'Is it?'

'No, it's Patrick, but you know what I mean.'

'I do,' said Ed.

'OK then. Good talk. Bye.'

'Bye.'

'Oh, and Ed?'

'Yeah?'

'Remember: you can't spell "trust" without *us.*'

And that was that. He wouldn't suspect a thing. Of course, I felt bad for being so deceitful, but then I remembered that this was serious shit that we were dealing with. This was sticker collecting, and in this world, sometimes you have to bend the rules a little.

I knew that first-hand. At the age of about ten, I dropped a big batch of swaps on the playground, and as the wind whipped them into all four corners of the quad, friends and enemies alike swarmed all over them, and ~~Hoovered~~ vacuumed them up. It wasn't fair, but that's the game.

For the next month, until my meeting with Scott, Anna and I spent almost every day with each other. I had numerous opportunities – really romantic ones, like where we were by some nice trees, or it wasn't raining, or the adverts were on – to finally tell her how I felt about her. But time after time, I was bottling it. Even as I began to slowly accumulate more and more of my stuff at her flat, I still had an irrational fear she might turn around and laugh in my face if I told her I was properly in love with her.

So while the days counted down to my meeting with Scott, we watched some football[36] and some Olympics (actually, Anna watched *none* of the Olympics, but she made me promise not to include that particular nugget of information in the book. And I intend to keep that promise. Which is why I've written this bit in brackets, which as we all know is visual whispering).

On 28 June, Henry VIII's birthday, I sent Ed a picture of his favourite monarch. He told me it was littered with historical inaccuracies (trainers, digital watch, machine gun, YOLO baseball hat) and promised to send a list of amendments through. A couple more letters arrived for me at Anna's flat. They both contained a photograph of Peter Atherton. I texted Jay and told him I hoped he was running out of swaps to send me.

* * * * *

6 July 2012
Friday

I met Scott in a coffee shop. We settled down with our drinks on opposite sides of a small table near the back and I told him the story so far.

I told him how my conversations with Philippe and Keith and Gary and Stuart had led me to realise something about my relationship with football, and the game itself. I told him how I was slowly realising that, away from the obvious financial

. . . .

36 Anna developed a brilliant technique for appearing interested in the game even if she actually wasn't watching. She would look up, and shout 'wide!' or 'give it!' or 'feet!' It was surprisingly effective.

and superficial changes to the game in the past two decades, something else had been happening.

Football, I argued, was less fun. Some of the romance that seemed to characterise my relationship with the game during my sticker album days had gone. And that, I told him, was the reason I was here, talking to him right now – to rediscover some of that feeling. It was also the reason I had parked in Philippe Albert's driveway[37] and stroked Gary Penrice's dog[38] in recent weeks.

Scott thought I was wrong. Football, particularly the Premier League, was in fine fettle. He insinuated that maybe I was over-reacting. I threw a coffee cup into a ceiling fan, punched a waiter in his mouth, then set fire to myself and told him I never, ever over-reacted.

Once the fire brigade/police/the National Society for the Prevention of Cruelty to Animals had sorted the situation (the sound of the cup smashing against the fan startled a sleeping beagle), we talked football.

It was interesting. But because I'm disorganised and easily distracted, I forgot that I was now contractually obliged to write a book about all this. I should have been asking more specific questions, but I wasn't, and the conversation got away from me.

It turned into a bit of a heated discussion about all sorts of 'proper' football topics that David Conn *et al* (Latin!) have covered in much greater depth and with far greater concision and eloquence and competence than I ever could. Things like finance and greed and football's role in society and what-not.

But to cut a long story short, Scott (who I was thrilled to discover was a lovely chap, highly intelligent and interesting and persuasive, not to mention ruddy good company) and I (who I was thrilled to discover after a series of expensive and confidence-shattering focus groups was not even *one* of those things) disagreed on *most* things when it came to football. For example – I borrowed an opinion from Philippe Albert and Gary Penrice, and said this:

'The Premier League is boring and predictable and increasingly defensive.'
• • • • • • •

37 Not a euphemism.
38 Not a euphemism.

To which Scott said this:

'I think the Premier League is something to be *really* proud of. The Premier League is *the* league. English football is not that great, but the Premier League is. The product is incredible. It is the best league in the world. Fair enough, La Liga might have the best three or four players and the best two teams in the world, but the Premier League is the best league in the world. It's the most entertaining and exciting.

'You go to a game and you're not 100 per cent sure of the result and that's true of the Premier League. Just look at how the league ended last season [2011/12 when Man City scored twice in injury time to beat QPR]. It was incredible.

'And this season [2012/13], there could feasibly be four teams winning the Premier League. And the standard has improved so much – you'd rather watch two mid-table teams now than mid-table teams from 15 years ago.'

Another example – I parroted something Keith Curle had said to me, and told Scott this:

'The Premier League is bad for the game as a whole. It is too far removed from the rest of British football. It is too powerful.'

Scott shot back with:

'There is a danger people are *too* obsessed with the Premier League and the gap is too big between the Premier League and the rest of English football. It is there on it's own – to say it's not a part of English football isn't quite right – but the Premier League *is* somewhat separate. It controls the game in this country.

'And obviously a lot of smaller clubs beneath the Premier League are in financial problems at the moment. The rich do have to look after the poor to a point, but clubs beneath the Premier League have to take more personal responsibility.

'If the Premier League worried about the lower leagues, the product would suffer and it's a simple scenario: if we want the best league in the world, then from the Premier League's point of view, [a separation between the Premier and Football Leagues] is a price that has to be paid. It is collateral damage. To get to where we are now, we've had to make sacrifices. Has it been worth it? I think so.

'And should a Man United fan even *care* about an Aldershot or whoever going out of business? Potentially they should, but do they? No, and I think it's a lot to ask anyone to care about other clubs; to ask them to think about football in general instead of just their own team.

'And listen: I know how important lower league football is in this country. You don't see crowds like we have in the third and fourth and non-league tiers anywhere else in the world. I played in the Championship and League 1 and I've seen how different life is. I've seen the countless number of players working their socks off for one- and two-year contracts; players who don't know where the game is going to take them and their families; players who know when they retire, they will have to start another career.

'That opened my eyes to the other end of the game, because I spent most of my time in the Premier League. At Rotherham in the Championship, I had to take my own kit to wash it. We had no gym, no canteen – it was back to the old school.

'But football fans are all the same, aren't they? "As long as my club is alright, who cares?" – that's the attitude, isn't it? Clubs [outside the Premier League] have to realise they're on their own. They're all chasing the riches of the Premier League, but they have to cut their cloth.'

Then I remembered something Stuart Ripley had said and borrowed that:

'Football is less accessible now than when I was a kid. It's prohibitively expensive to watch. The game is removed from the real world.'

Again, Scott countered with this:

'I think more affluent people, older people are going now and – for the want of a better word – the lower classes and families are getting priced out, who are historically football's audience. But everything – and *everyone* – has to evolve. Those people might not be able to afford to go now, but they can watch the game on TV now, and that's great.

'More people are watching than ever before. That's a fact. I think the game is *more* accessible because you don't have to go to the ground to watch your team now. People can watch their team *more*, not less.

'You don't even need to be in the same city, you can be at the other end of the country and support your team. Sky do football so well and that's brought more people into the game – people who maybe didn't even used to watch the game. It's not ideal that some people can only watch on telly, but it's better than 25 years ago when if you didn't get to the game you saw nothing.

'I can't deny it – football is everywhere now, but that's only because it's so popular. The coverage of the game is expanding because it needs to meet the demand. If people didn't want more football on the television, nobody would provide it. If you don't want to watch it, you can turn over.'

I shook my head, though I was enjoying the exchange, and moved on to my next (borrowed) point. I remembered something Stuart and Gary had said to me during our meetings.

'The players are disconnected from the real world,' I said. 'The money they earn can be a corrupting and distorting influence. The idea of "playing for the joy of the game" has gone from the modern game. True, or false?'

'It's true that if you're a Premier League player now, you're set up for life. A Premier League player nowadays earns enough to never have to work again, once they're retired. But there are still rounded people playing the game now. Footballers haven't changed, I don't think.

'Maybe, in the past, there was more room for players to have a bit of character. I went on nights out with journalists as a player and that would never happen now. I played at a time when I earned decent money, but could fly under the radar a bit. Back then, players could basically have a bit more fun. It wasn't so regimented.

'But it's always been the case that some players are *just* concerned with making a living, and some players *don't* love the game. But the majority, though, still play because they love the game, and the game will never be about the money for them. It's that old cliche of "if they weren't getting paid, they would still be playing football with their mates".

'You say that players are too far removed from fans, but people know more about the players now than ever before, because of the increased coverage of football. Nothing has changed in terms of the relationship between the fans and the players. There was always pressure from the crowd; there was always abuse. Being at Chelsea, I remember world-class players getting stick.'

Scott knew his stuff. He was a better journalist than me, by a factor of loads. And he was a committed Premierleagueophile – a word I just made up and added to my Microsoft Word custom dictionary – which means 'a person who believes the Premier League is the best league in the world'. I was not one of those. I disagreed with him on a fundamental level, but I was happy to have met Scott. I liked him.

In a funny way, talking to him re-emphasised the whole point of this little adventure. It didn't matter that Scott had a different opinion to me on certain things. It was good to talk to someone who enjoyed all the Premier League had to offer, and truly bought into it. It was obvious that he still loved football, and he still enjoyed watching it. I felt a little pang of jealousy that I couldn't be a little more like him.

Now, if this was a Wes Anderson film, a whimsical song would start playing, while I stared wistfully over some beautifully-shot scenery. It would be something acoustic and lo-fi and self-consciously kooky, with a really lame title like *The (very short) Ballad of Scott Minto*. For example. And it would probably go something like this:

```
          'The (very short) Ballad of Scott Minto'
          Words and Music by Adam Carroll-Smith.

        G
No, we don't agree on many things,

            Am
In fact we don't agree on any thing,

        D                       C                       G
But we both love football and that's the important thing.


[WHISTLE SOLO.]


[GLOCKENSPIEL SOLO.]


Fade out.


Fade back in.


[ANOTHER WHISTLE SOLO.]


Fade out again.
```

'Maybe you're right,' Scott said, as we finished our drinks, and I stopped singing the lyrics to *T(vs)BOSM* in my head. 'Maybe *something* has gone. Maybe something fundamental has changed. But you need to balance it out. To get to where we are now, we've had to make sacrifices. Has it been worth it? I think so.

'I think you're in the minority in thinking that somehow football has lost some of it's soul and adventure. It's nostalgia playing tricks. It's the same thing as when you think of an old girlfriend. When you think back, you just conveniently forget the bad times. Ask yourself this: has football changed, or has Hugh changed?'

Jokes, 31–33.

Roque Santa Cruz, *n.* a turbulent sea holiday for overweight seasonal workers.

CONCACAF, *n.* A delicious coffee made from conkers.[39]

Which West Brom player was also a movie star as a child? Gareth McAuley-Culkin.

· · · · · · ·
39 Awful.

Nineteen

I was pretty sure I had misheard Scott.

'Pardon?' I said. 'Has football changed, or has *Hugh* changed?'

'*You*. Has football changed, or have *you* changed?' said Scott. Which made a lot more sense. Scott got up and went to what the Americans would call a bathroom, but everyone else would call the toilets. I thought about what he had just asked me.

Had football changed, or had *I* changed?
Had football changed, or had *I* changed?
Had football changed, or had *I* changed?
(At this point I got distracted.)
Did Hal from *Space Odyssey* have a surname? I think he did.
Had football changed, or had *I* changed?
I'm pretty sure his full name was Hal Nine-Thousand. A fellow double-barreller!
Had football changed, or had *I* changed?
You know, I would never take a job where my title started with the word 'human'.
Had football changed, or had *I* changed?
'*Human Cannonball*' – too dangerous.
Had football changed, or had *I* changed?
'*Human Torch*' – also too dangerous.
Had football changed, or had *I* changed?
'*Human Resources Manager*' – would rather be set on fire or shot out of a cannon.
Had football changed, or had *I* changed?
I could use emotional blackmail. Or unemotional blackmail (like emotional blackmail, but with less crying, more guns).
Had football changed, or …

It was a pretty good question and I wasn't quite ready for it. I really was getting distracted pretty easily. While Scott was still away from the table, I re-focused my mind and made a couple of mental lists which I hoped might help me answer his question.

LIST #1:
THINGS I HADN'T DONE IN 1996 WHICH I HAVE DONE SINCE AND WHICH SEEM LIKE PRETTY IMPORTANT THINGS NOW I HAVE DONE THEM AND SHOW HOW MUCH I HAVE CHANGED (provisional title).

1. Learned to swim
2. Kissed a girl
3. Drank (drunk? drinked? Probably 'drinked') a beer
4. Listened to Mogwai or Grandaddy or The Twilight Sad or Pavement or Daniel Johnston or John Coltrane or anyone good, basically
5. Ever watched/listened to any work by Steve Martin, Louis C.K., Jerry Seinfeld, Demetri Martin, Aziz Ansari, Tina Fey, Amy Poehler, Stewart Lee, Milton Jones, Reginald D Hunter, Steven Wright, Daniel Kitson, Simon Munnery, Dylan Moran or any of the comedians I love now
6. Tried pesto
7. Driven a car
8. Been employed
9. Got some qualifications
10. Had my heart broken by a lady
11. Moved into own home
12. Drinked a chai latte

I could have gone on, but I didn't. Scott was on his way back to the table. I quickly moved on to mental list #2 as he sat back down.

LIST #2:
THINGS I USED TO ENJOY DOING IN 1996 WHICH I HAVE SINCE STOPPED DOING AND WHOSE REMOVAL FROM MY LIST OF INTERESTS ALSO SHOWS HOW MUCH I HAVE CHANGED AND MATURED (even more provisional title).

1. Used to enjoy *Big Break* (cancelled)
2. Used to enjoy WWF (fake)
3. Used to enjoy *Baywatch* (fake, cancelled)

Again, the list could have gone on, but the evidence was irrefutable. Or undeniable. Or indisputable. Basically, there was evidence lying around the place, and all of it pointed to the same conclusion. Scott was right. I *had* changed a lot. I was older, wiser, marginally more financially independent, and I had a beautiful girlfriend I definitely wanted to marry once I had mustered the courage to even tell her that I was totally in love with her.

But football, I quickly realised, had changed even more. And most crucially, while I *liked* most of the changes *I* had made, football, it seemed, had changed for the worse. It was greedy and heartless and false and boring and it took itself way too seriously. Like an estate agent. It hadn't, I told Scott, always been like this. When I was a kid collecting *Premier League* 96 stickers the first time around, football was united and inclusive, fun and exciting.

Again, Scott did not agree. 'You say football felt more united in 1996, but is that realistic? There *wasn't* this great community feel to football then.

'Yes, Euro 96 brought the whole country together, but only in the way people all play tennis during Wimbledon and then forget about it a week later. If we'd have got to the semi-finals of the European Championships this year, it would have felt the same – like everyone was facing the same way. I think there is a correlation with you being a Portsmouth fan ...' I had told Scott that I supported Pompey while we queued for our coffees. '... If Pompey were still in the top league and money-rich, would you feel the same? Would you still think the game was less fun if Pompey weren't in such trouble?'

'I don't know.'

'I don't think you would. Pompey won the FA Cup in 2008, right?'

I nodded. Not because I'm a yes man, but because Scott was being factually precise.

'Would you swap that win – which was won paying wages that have ruined the club – for stability now?'

I shrugged. 'I'm not sure. At the final whistle, I *did* say that I didn't care if the club slid down the divisions, because that moment was such an overwhelming rush of emotion.'

'Exactly!' cried Scott. 'Now, if the club doesn't go out of business, if the club ends up surviving through all this, then it was the right decision to spend that money and win that trophy.'

'Maybe,' I shrugged.

SCOTT MINTO

With that, we wrapped the conversation up. I had work to do, and Scott had to be elsewhere. I pulled my camera out and took his picture.

I did a few calculations on a scrap of paper and was elated to discover I was now, mathematically speaking, just one sticker away from completion. My album was (529 ÷ 530) x 100% full. All that remained was Lars Bohinen. And I knew *exactly* where to find him.

On the way back from my meeting with Scott, I pulled in at a service station and did some work. '*Work*'. Rosh had sent me a few e-mails, but thankfully, my unscheduled morning off had gone relatively unnoticed. After a few hours, I got a little bored. I surfed my way on to eBay and tried to find one of the remaining eight stickers Ed still needed. But after a fruitless half-hour of searching – there were loads on there, each priced at *way* more than you would ever expect, just none that Ed needed – I decided I needed to be a little more precise in my hunting. I called Ed.

'Hi Ed, it's Adam – no time to chat – this is just a quick message about the eight stickers you need.'

'Four.'

'What?'

'Yeah, it's four now. Another package arrived.'

'You've broken the truce!' I shouted, apparently outraged that Ed had done exactly what I had literally just done. But at least I had the decency to lie about it.

'No I haven't,' he replied. 'I bought these before the truce had been agreed. It's just taken a while for them to arrive. The package came from Ireland or somewhere.'

'Rubbish!' I moaned. 'This is improper. Unproper. It's not proper!'

'It *is* proper. I have broken no rules.'

'You have,' I said.

'Have not,' said Ed.

'Have.'

'Have not.'

'Have.'

'Have not.'

'Have not,' I said, trying to catch Ed out.

'I know,' he replied, quite cleverly. I admitted defeat immediately.

'Fine. But I think you should give me Lars Bohinen now.'

'No.'

'Fine. Then I think you should tell me which four stickers you need.'

Ed told me he still needed the Bolton kit shiny, the lower half of David Ginola, Richard Hall from Southampton and the Wimbledon programme sticker. I asked him which one he needed the most. He told me that was a stupid question, and put the phone down.

And that was the last time Ed and I spoke about stickers for a month. Until the Olympics ended and the truce lifted, Ed and I said not a single word to each other about stickers. We both set aside our personal ambitions, and enjoyed one of the finest sporting summers ever.

Actually, I did my very best, more or less every day, to complete the album without Ed knowing. I called Lars Bohinen every day, but his phone was switched off 90 per cent of the time. When it wasn't off, he wasn't answering. He hadn't re-followed me on Twitter either. The chances of meeting him suddenly seemed the exact opposite of Andy Reid (i.e. very, very slim). That meant just two options remained – I could pack my bags and head for Norway, or I could try and get the Lars Bohinen sticker from Ed.

I had a preference, of course. I had already been to Belgium and Orpington on a whim, and both times, I had been forced to turn around and head for home empty-handed. So the sticker swap was Plan A. Just turning up at Oslo airport and asking for 'directions to Lars Bohinen's house' was Plan Z, even if, right now, there were no plans B, C, D, E, F, G, H, I, J, K, L, M, N, O, P, Q, R, S, T, U, V, W, X or Y.

(Don't skim that list, by the way. Read it properly. There is a joke hidden in there.)

But there were problems with Plan A, too. I scanned eBay every day for the stickers Ed needed, but never found anything useful. And without a sticker to swap, Ed would never give me the Lars sticker.

I was out of ideas on how to get the album over the line, but Anna – the wonderful, clever, inventive Anna – had a few more. She wrote an e-mail to Bolton Wanderers, asking them if they had any surplus *Premier League 96* shinies lying around the office. She made me send a tweet to David Ginola asking him to forward on a picture of the lower half of his body. She found out that Richard Hall worked for Colchester United Football Club, so we sent them an e-mail about wanting to meet up with Richard sometime soon.

She also suggested I buy a random Wimbledon programme and make my own sticker by taking a photograph of it. I told her Ed would probably veto it unless it was the *exact* programme featured on the actual sticker in the collection. I called Ed and asked him. He said he would definitely veto it unless it was the *exact* programme featured on the actual sticker in the collection. Then he told me some spurious fact about Henry VIII and I put the phone down immediately.

And last, but by no means least, Anna suggested I tear the thin slip of card – the one inviting the reader to buy their remaining few stickers direct from Merlin at a cost of 6p each, up to a maximum of 50 stickers – out from under the staples in the middle pages of *Premier League 96,* and send it off. Of all of her ideas, this was the longest shot. Longer even than asking Bolton Wanderers if they had a 16-year-old shiny-backed sticker sitting in a drawer.

For one thing, I was fairly sure Merlin didn't even exist as a company anymore, and if they did, they had probably moved offices since 1996. But I did it anyway. I filled in the details of Ed's four stickers. I put the card in an envelope, wrote the address of Merlin headquarters on the front, and slipped a cheque for 24p inside, along with a small note explaining why I was sending this letter 16 years late.

I put a stamp on the envelope, and then I posted that envelope in a post box, where it sat with a load of other envelopes (and small packages) until a man (or woman) from the Post Office came and took the envelopes (and small packages) away. Standard letter-sending procedure, basically. I have probably over-described it.

But that's what I did. And then, I waited.

For Lars.

For David Ginola.

For Bolton Wanderers.

For Colchester United.

For Merlin (the sticker manufacturer, not the wizard).

For any of them, really.

But mainly, for Lars.

I stared at his name in my phonebook and willed him to call me. He didn't. Because it was the only option I still hadn't tried, I sent him a text message. It was short and straight-to-the-point, like a Gareth Barry pass, only straight-to-the-point too. I introduced myself as 'the guy from Twitter' and told Lars once again why I needed to meet with him. I over-sold this book and told him I was writing 'an important story about football' which I wanted him to be a part of. I pressed send, my fingers crossed behind the back of the phone for luck. But even as I did, it seemed likelier that a probably defunct sticker manufacturer would send me 24p worth of stickers through the post, than it would be that Lars would reply.

(Did you spot the hidden joke? Only five per cent of readers spot the joke.)

* * * * *

13 August 2012
Monday

It was the first day after the end of the truce. Ed called with news. He had found a Richard Hall sticker online, and purchased it, which took him down to three required. Later in the day, he called with more news. Against the odds, he had found David Ginola's legs which, again, was a relief. I was beginning to feel uncomfortable writing all those e-mails and letters to his agents and management and what-not, asking them for 'a photograph of the lower half of David's body, preferably in shorts, with a ball'. Ed told me he now needed only two stickers – the Wimbledon programme and the Bolton kit shiny – to finish his album.

'I now need only two stickers – the Wimbledon programme and the Bolton kit shiny – to finish my album,' said Ed, telling me what I've just told you, as I told you he had.

'That's true. Well done. I am happy for you. I truly feel the human emotion of happiness towards you,' I lied.

'So now we're nip and tuck, neck and neck, level pegging, equal, tied,' said Ed.

He said that, because he thought we were. Now, you and I know different. But we are the only ones who do. If I had remembered that I had recently deceived Ed, I probably would have said something like this:

'Yes Ed, you're right. Due to the fact that, like you, I did not break the agreed truce, I **also** need two more stickers – Scott Minto and Lars Bohinen. Now, please tell me more interesting historical facts about King Henry VIII of England.'

But what I actually said, was this:

'Well, no, I only need one more, don't I?'

'What!?'

'Yeah. Lars Bohinen,' I replied, because at this point I still hadn't quite realised what I was saying, and what sordid revelation I was dumbly emptying from my mouth hole into Ed's ear balls.

'But I thought you had to meet Scott Minto?!'

'Yeah I did, but …'

And *there* it is – the moment that I realised what I was saying. And as soon as I realised, I stopped saying it. I stopped and wished and hoped that if I just said nothing else for a little while, Ed might move on and change the subject. It was the audio equivalent of standing still in the face of a T-Rex attack. It didn't work.

'Adam, why have you stopped talking? Finish that sentence, please,' said Ed.

'No, no, I was mistaken. I *do* still need two. I miscounted.'

'You miscounted? You tried to count to *two*, but you got stuck on *one*?'

'Exactly. I'm embarrassed.'

'Tell me the truth. Did you break the terms of the ceasefire?'

'No.'

'Did you meet Scott Minto during an agreed time of non-combat, during which we had both agreed to take a temporary break from collecting our stickers?'

'No.'

'How many stickers do you still require to complete your album?'

'Two.'

'I will ask you again: how many stickers do you still require to complete your album?'

'Two.'

'How many?'

'Two.'

'Two?'

'Two.'

'Was Scott a nice guy?'

'I don't know Ed, I haven't yet had the pleasure of meeting him.'

'Bullshit.'

'It's true. I still need to meet Lars Bohinen *and* Scott Minto.'

'I *know* you're lying.'

'How?! I mean, no I'm not.'

'Yes you are. How many stickers do you still need!'

'Two.'

'One.'

'Two.'

'One.'

'Two.'

'One.'

'Two.'

'Two?'

'Yes, two. Definitely two.'

'Adam, if you just tell me, honestly, that you met Scott Minto and broke the terms of our truce, I will not be angry. I will not withhold this Lars Bohinen sticker from you. I will still swap it for one of the remaining stickers I need. I just want you to tell me,' said Ed, his voice changing from a raspy growl to a soft and soothing coo. 'Did you meet Scott Minto during the truce?'

Ed seemed genuine, and with one eye on the fact I would have to write this little exchange up in the book you are now reading, I decided to move things along. The whole 'Two! One! Two! One! Two! One!' thing was dragging on a bit. I remembered the old adage about honesty being the best policy.

'Alright,' I said, my voice devoid of emotion, like a robot or Michael Owen. 'Yes, I did.'

'WHAT?' shrieked Ed.

It was at this point I decided that honesty was no longer the best policy.

'Only joking,' I said quickly.

Ed, angry and relieved at what he thought was a cruel wind-up, called me a dick over and over. Rounding down to the nearest round number, I think he said it a million times. He was right, but for the wrong reasons. I felt guilty. More than that, I felt an overwhelming urge to make amends.

Although actually, it *wasn't* an overwhelming urge. It was an urge which I felt, then stifled, ignored, and finally killed and buried under the proverbial patio of my mind. I cackled to myself like an evil genius for four or five hours, because this was a battle. A competition. And I was in it to win it.

And anyway, Ed would never know of my deception. Or at least he wouldn't know about it until he read it in this book, by which point it would be too late for him to complain. It was the perfect crime. I temporarily worried that maybe all this was bad karma which might come back to bite me in the arse, but then I ate a doughnut and forgot all about it.

(There was no hidden joke in the alphabet earlier. Sorry.)

* * * * *

14 August 2012
The following morning

1000 hrs

Check e-mails. Actually, woke up first, then checked e-mails. Three new messages.

Two very forward messages promising 'opportunities to grow'. *Deleted.* (Fingers burned before. Wise to the scams now.)

One from Rosh. *Boring.*

1020 hrs

Put bread in toaster.

1025 hrs

Check Twitter account. No tweets from Lars Bohinen.

1045 hrs

Write another text to Lars. Notice he is now listed as a contact on WhatsApp. Send him a message on there, too.

1100 hrs

Period of extended sitting around begins. Toilet breaks at regular intervals. Make mental note to get it fixed. Make second mental note to improve pun work.

1105 hrs

Check old mental notes. Realise I have made the above mental notes before. The exact same ones. Make third mental note to action mental notes quicker in future.

1300 hrs

Period of extended sitting around ends, but only because a period of joyous celebration begins. My phone has received a text message. Periods of air-punching and whooping and Robbie Keane-style cartwheels also begin. Something wonderful has happened. Lars has replied to my text! He has sent me his e-mail address!

1315 hrs
Periods of joyous celebration, air-punching, whooping and Robbie Keane-style cartwheels all end, so I can send an e-mail to Lars. Explain, in as much detail as I can, why I need to meet him. Explain that I have already met Stuart and Gary and Keith and Philippe and Scott and hope that this will demonstrate that I am not a complete mentalist.

Remember that Stuart had asked me to say 'hi' if I ever ended up speaking to Lars. Write 'Stuart Ripley says "hi", by the way!' at the end of the e-mail. Feel good that I am reconnecting two former team-mates. Click send. Period of refreshing my e-mails every five minutes and waiting for a reply begins.

1320 hrs
No reply.

1325 hrs
No reply.

1330 hrs
No reply.

1335 hrs
No reply. (Although I can feel one coming on.)

1340 hrs
No reply. (It was wind.)

1345 hrs
No reply.

1350 hrs
No reply.

1355 hrs
No reply.

1400 hrs
No reply.

1405 hrs
No reply.

1410 hrs
No reply.

1415 hrs
No reply.

1420 hrs
No reply.

1425 hrs
No reply.

1430 hrs
No reply.

1435 hrs
No reply.

1436 hrs
'Hi Adam, I've been busy lately, but you can call me later this afternoon. Regards, Lars.'

Art, 7.

CROSS BAR.

Twenty

THE MESSAGE looked genuine, but I didn't allow myself to get too complacent, or to start celebrating prematurely. I checked that the e-mail was definitely from Lars, and not some elaborate hoax. Then I double-checked that the e-mail was definitely from Lars, and not some elaborate hoax. Then I triple-checked that the e-mail was definitely from Lars, and not some elaborate hoax. And only after all that was I certain that the e-mail was definitely from Lars, and not some elaborate hoax.

The e-mail was genuine. Lars *had* replied. The last of my six was in my grasp.

This was huge; as huge as Olivier Giroud's [*redacted*]. At least, that's the rumour, anyway. [*redacted*] inches, allegedly.

After so many months of striving, I finally allowed myself to dream. The album was going to be complete. I was going to finish, and finish ahead of Ed, too. Sure, once I was finished, I would probably have to think about why exactly I had done all this in the first place, but that was a conversation I would have with myself at a later date. Right now, it was time to bask in the near-certain success I was about to enjoy.

I called Anna and told her my sticker book quest was nearly at an end. I told her in great detail the sort of celebration I wanted to have once I had met Lars and taken his picture. I told her I was torn between wall-mounting the album in an ornate wood and gold frame and creating a sort of lasting shrine to it's completeness, or ritualistically pushing it out to sea on a burning barge and drinking heavily to toast its long-overdue conquering. Anna preferred a third suggestion – her own – that I just throw it into the sea, and then move on. I preferred my ideas.

I called Ed, too – not to gloat, necessarily, although I didn't trust myself not to turn a little gloaty at some point in the conversation. As it turned out, Ed was very gracious in defeat, even if he did mutter something beneath his breath about this whole contest not being over quite yet. But deep down, he knew it was, and so did I. Now that Lars was on board, nothing could stand in my way.

I invited him to the shrine unveiling/Norse sea burial down in Southsea, but he said he was busy. I resisted the temptation to say 'busy looking for stickers, I bet!' but I felt as though I was thinking it so loudly that Ed must have heard. I apologised anyway.

After a few minutes of chatting, Ed and I parted on good terms. I promised – sincerely – that I would find a way to help him get hold of the final two stickers he needed, so we could both proudly say we had completed our albums. Ed muttered away beneath his breath again, and I felt a little bad for him. He had wanted to complete his album before I completed mine every bit as desperately as I wanted to finish mine before he finished his.

But before I could feel too much sympathy, I thought back to all those childhood disappointments – those crushing blows delivered on a windswept Pompey playground by the big kid with the pig nose who had just moved down from Manchester, the one who had millions of swaps, but refused to help me out with an Oldham shiny and who blatantly stole my spare Ian Rush during break time, you know who you are, you dick – and I realised that I had earned this success. I had a right to enjoy it. But first, I had to arrange it. I called Lars, as instructed, with a view to scheduling our all-important meeting.

The first time I called, he didn't answer.

But that was OK.

I replied to his text and told him I was calling him.

Then I called him again.

He didn't answer that time, either.

I popped my phone on the side, and left it alone for a few minutes.

When I returned to it, I found Lars had yet to return my calls.

Or text me back.

So I dialled his number again.

The call went straight to answerphone.

I didn't leave a message.

I dialled again.

No answer.

I went out for a walk.

For an hour.

I left my phone at home.

I convinced myself that Lars would have called by the time I got back.

Or texted.

Maybe e-mailed.

He hadn't called.

Or texted.

Or e-mailed.

So I called him again.

By now, it was no longer the afternoon.

It was the evening.

I didn't have a mandate to call in the evening, but I did it anyway.

The phone went straight to voice-mail.

I still didn't leave a message.

I called again, and again, and again.

Once.

Twice.

Three times.

A voice-mail.

And then, I gave up.

Because this was no accident.

This was not a coincidence.

This was retribution.

Not from Ed – not because I'd met Scott Minto behind his back.

But from a peculiar footballing force.

The same one responsible for David Batty's missed penalty at France 98: mockers.

At France 98, a combination of Barry Davies and Kevin Keegan were responsible for tempting mockers. But my first experience with the hateful m-word came years before, way back in 1992, when Pompey reached the semi-finals of the FA Cup, and were drawn to play Liverpool at Highbury.

I wasn't there in north London but sat at home, watching the match live on television with my family. Pompey, much to the surprise of just about everyone, kept the Reds at bay. The match finished goalless after 90 minutes.

I asked my dad what came next. 'Hopefully a Liverpool goal,' he said. Scummer. A wonderful scummer whom I love very much. But still, a scummer.

The first half of extra time also ended 0-0 and penalties looked certain until five minutes into the second half. A hoofed Pompey clearance ended up at Darren Anderton's feet in the inside-right channel, and after a leggy run – what other type is there, though? – he fired a weak shot towards Bruce Grobbelaar in the Liverpool goal. The ball did nothing, neither dip nor curl nor bobble, but somehow it squirmed through Grobbelaar's grasp before nestling gently in the back of the net.

The Pompey fans at Highbury leapt into full-throated delirium. Back home, I sprang from my cross-legged position in front of the TV and dived headlong over the sofa cushions in excitement. I kissed the badge on my chest. My dad sat passive in the corner, stubborn in his misguided Southampton loyalty. My wonderful mum split her time between celebration and consolation. That is the sort of woman she is.

For the next few minutes, Pompey held firm in the face of concerted Liverpool pressure. Now, just five minutes stood between Pompey and a trip to the FA Cup Final. I was excited, so I decided to state what seemed obvious: Pompey were going to win, the club was going to Wembley, and we were going to beat Sunderland in the final and win the entire competition. It was undeniable.

Or so I thought. Seconds later, Liverpool won a free kick on the edge of the Portsmouth area. John Barnes's curling effort beat the wall and struck Alan Knight's left-hand post, sending the ball trickling along the goal line in agonising super slo-mo. The Pompey defence watched it roll, their feet and minds frozen from exhaustion. Ronnie Whelan tapped the ball home from inches. I burst into tears (figuratively).

Pompey's chance at glory had gone. The game ended in a draw and eight days later, the Blues lost the replay at Villa Park on penalties. I felt partially responsible. I should have kept my mouth shut.

In the years since, I have taken great care not to repeat my mistake. I have held my tongue and resisted the urge to say anything during a football match which sounds like corrosive, presumptuous complacency. No matter the score, until the final whistle blows my belief that Pompey can still lose is as unbending as Jonathan Woodgate trying to touch his toes.

But now, stupidly, I had broken my own rule. I had been bold where I should have been cautious. I thought again that this was perhaps karma for the wilful deceit I had shown in meeting Scott Minto behind Ed's back. But then I drank a milkshake and forgot all about that. This was definitely mockers at work.

That night, while Anna and I ate dinner at the flat and I tried (unsuccessfully) to just tell her how wonderful she was and how in love with her I was, Ed called. I ignored it. He called again. I continued to ignore him.

So he sent me a text.

Call me.

That's all it said.

But I did not.

So he texted me again.

Seriously, call me.

That's all it said.

Pretty similar in tone and content to the first one.

But, seriously, I did not call him.

Still, he continued to call.

He called again, and again, and again.

So I turned my phone off.

He didn't seem to call as often once I did that.

Half-an-hour later, I turned it back on.

A new text from Ed was waiting for me.

I didn't read it.

There was a new voice-mail too.

I didn't listen to it.

I just ate the rest of the delicious homemade lemon drizzle cake Anna had made,

And watched another episode of *The Office*,

The American one, which is really good.
Maybe even better than the English one, actually.
And fell asleep on the sofa with the woman I loved.

* * * * *

15 August 2012
Wednesday

The following morning, another envelope, addressed to me, arrived at Anna's flat. I knew what it was, but this time, the arrival of this letter had happier consequences. Anna suggested that this whole 'post arriving for me' thing had given her an idea. I may as well make it official, and move in. I accepted, very quickly.

As Anna and I celebrated this tremendously exciting news, I realised just how huge a step this was for us. This, surely, meant we were now a proper, grown-up couple. Soon, we would be doing weekly food shops together, discussing furniture options and saying things like 'we really should get a Dualit toaster, even if they do cost £70, because the bagel option is just superb'.

I thought back to the night I met Anna. Back then, I was an immature, slightly lost and confused little chap. I didn't want to buy food a week in advance or talk about G-Plan sideboards. I was quite happy with the £11 toaster I already had. All this moving in with Anna stuff made me feel slightly more mature, and much less lost and confused. Anna was responsible for that sea change in me. I was, however, still quite short, but there wasn't really anything Anna could do about that, so I didn't hold it against her.

Anna made me feel happier than I had ever felt before. She had supported me while I wasted countless hours on this stupid sticker album thing, and now all I wanted to do was finish it, so we could spend more time together. *That*, I realised, was the important thing. The album had, in a weird way, brought Anna and I closer together. But now it was a third wheel. It would have to go, and soon.

Anna and I ate breakfast together on the sofa, and as we spooned away mouthfuls of muesli and forkfuls of egg on toast, I opened the envelope with my name on it. It felt heavier than the previous letters from Jay. I eased it open, and sure enough, pulled out a neatly folded letter. I unfolded it and began to read. I got a few words in and nearly fell off my chair.

Dear Adam,

I hope you don't mind, but I got your address from a mutual friend of ours. I think you can probably guess which one!

I have been intrigued by your sticker album quest for a while, but now I am keen to help. Please find enclosed a couple of items I hope will be of use.

Good luck, and happy collecting.

Best wishes,

Alan Risley-Tan

Alan Risley-Tan? Alan? Risley-Tan? Who the hell was that? I tried to think if I knew anyone by that name. I didn't. I tried to recall if I'd met anyone called Alan recently. And then it hit me. *Oh shit*, I thought to myself.

I *had* met someone called Alan.

The juggler in Belgium.

His name was Alan, wasn't it?

I went back to page 93 and checked.

It *was* Alan. It had to be him. And if it was, I might have to rethink my whole attitude towards jugglers. Maybe they weren't all bad.

I snatched up the envelope and shook it out on to the floor. Three stickers fluttered out. The first was Peter Schmeichel. Not that helpful. The second was Peter Atherton. Again, again, again. I showed Anna and she looked a little spooked. Before she met me, she didn't even know Peter Atherton existed, and now small photographs of his face were arriving, more or less every other week, at her address.

One sticker remained. It was face down on the carpet. All I could see was the number, 232, on the back. I recognised the number immediately, because for the past few weeks, it had been one I had spent a lot of time trying to find. I turned it over, and as I did, I heard the sound of stirring, emotionally-charged and very epic piano rock begin to play. It wasn't very good, but it suited the mood, which was joyous, because in my hand was a sticker that was worth its weight in gold. To me, but also, to someone else.

'So? Come on! What is it!' said Anna, clocking the twin looks of elation and astonishment on my face. I held the sticker up. Anna smiled.

'Is that …?'
'Yes,' I interrupted.
'And Ed still …?'
'Yes.'
'So shall we …?'
'Yes,' I said, grabbing my phone. 'Let's.'

* * * * *

FADE IN.

INT. FRONT ROOM – DAY

THE ROOM is brightly lit. Sun is pouring into the room from three large windows, through which we can see that the flat is a few storeys above street level. In the centre of the room is a coffee table, covered with books and magazines and plates of half-eaten breakfast food. In one corner is a table littered with craft stuff, fabric and a sewing machine. The television is on, but the sound is muted. ADAM and ANNA are sat, side-by-side, on a black leather sofa. They both look excited. ADAM is on his phone, waiting for someone on the other end to answer.

ADAM
Pick up, Ed. Pick up …

ANNA
Has he picked up?

ADAM
No.

(A beat)

ANNA
Now?

ADAM
ED!

ADAM is suddenly animated. The person on the other end of the phone, ED, has answered. We can only hear one side of the conversation.

ADAM
Ed, it's Adam. Yes, I'm good. Now listen, I have some big news for you.

(A beat)

No.

(A beat)

Nope.

(A beat)

Stop guessing.

(A beat)

Stop.

(A beat)

Just let me tell you my news!

ADAM picks up a sticker from a coffee table opposite the sofa.

ADAM
Guess what I'm holding in my hand *right now*?

(A beat)

No. Ed, why would I be holding that while I'm on the phone to you?

(A beat)

That's very funny, actually. That's genuinely hilarious. I'll be re-telling that. But seriously, guess what I'm holding. It's small, but *very* valuable.

(A beat)

I'm choosing to ignore that.

ADAM composes himself, as though he is about to say something of great magnitude and importance. He puts ED on loudspeaker. We can now hear both sides of the conversation.

ADAM
Ed, I've got the Wimbledon programme sticker.

ED
Shut up.

ADAM
I'm serious.

ED
The Wimbledon programme?

ADAM
The *Wimbledon* programme.

ED
The *Wimbledon programme*!

From the tinny phone speaker, we hear ED laughing riotously and whooping very loudly. He begins to chant 'USA! USA! USA!' for some reason. ADAM is smiling. A lot. He begins to run around the room, occasionally passing by ANNA and giving her a high-five. She too is smiling. A lot. After a minute or so, the noise quietens down, and ADAM sits back down on the sofa, beside ANNA.

ADAM
So … when are we going to …

ED chuckles warmly, then sighs deeply.

ED
Got.

ADAM
What?

ED
Did you know Henry VIII grew the English navy from five ships to over 60 ships during his reign?

ADAM
What do you mean, 'got'?!

ED
Oh. I've got it. I don't need it.

ADAM
But you just laughed riotously! You just whooped!

ED
I know.

ADAM
WHY?!

ED
I just really like Wimbledon.

ADAM
That's not fucking funny!

ANNA
(off camera)
It's *pretty* funny.

ED
Did you not get my voice-mail?

ADAM
No.

ED
Check my voice-mail.

ED puts the phone down suddenly. ADAM stands, motionless, in the centre of the room. He presses a few buttons on his phone, then holds it to his ear.

ANNA
So? What's happened?

ADAM
He's left me a voice-mail.

ANNA
Put it on loudspeaker.

ADAM puts the call on loudspeaker, even though ANNA does not use the magic word ('please'). ANNA moves closer to listen.

ED
(*through loudspeaker*)

Hello Adam. It is I, Ed. I have some news. Some *exciting* news. Well, it's exciting for *me*, anyway. I have found the final two stickers I need. I have bought them. They will be delivered to me by Monday. I'm sure you realise what this means. You are about to lose. I am about to win.

ED laughs for two or three minutes, then the message ends. The room is totally quiet.

ADAM
Bollocks.

FADE OUT.

Twenty and a half

Top secret morse code mini-chapter which you really should take the time to translate.

- .... / .. ... / .- / .... . -.-. .-. . - / -- . ...- --. . . .-.-.- / .... . -. -.. / -- . /
.- / - .-- . . - / -.-. --- -. - .- .. -. .. -. --. / - .... . / .--. .... -. .- .- .... . / .---- . .--.
..- .. ... -....- .---- . / -.... -. --- ... .-. ..--.. ----. / .- -. -.-. / .. / .-- .. .-..
.-.. / .... . -. -.. / -.-- --- ..- / .- / --- -. -.. .. -....- .- -....- .- -.--.- -. .. -. -.. /
-... .- .-. .- -.-- .. -. --. / --- ..-. / .--. .- --- .-.. --- / -- .- .-. -.-. .-.. -.. .. / .--. .. --- -.
-.-. .... .. -. --. / .- / .-.. -.. .. ... --- -. -. --..-- / --- .-. / .... --- -- --. . - -... .- . -. -. -. / .... ..
-- .. .-.. .- .-.-.- / --. --- --- ---... / .-... -.-. -.-. -.- .-.-.-

Jokes, 34–36.

Yeovil. Popular among rappers.

Grant Holt, *n.* What happened to students when tuition fees kicked in.

Commentators! Stop throwing the form book out of the window! Littering is a crime.

Twenty-one

16 August 2012
Thursday

'Hi Rosh, it's Adam.'

'Hi.'

'Listen – I need to take tomorrow off.'

'I know. Ed told me.'

'What did he tell you?'

'He told me you might need to take tomorrow off.'

'Oh.'

'Yeah. He also told me *why* you might need to take tomorrow off.'

'Oh.'

'And unfortunately, my answer is no …'

'Oh …'

'… because you need to come into the office. We have a client meeting.'

'Since when?'

'Since Ed booked it in this morning.'

'Sabotage!'

'And he's booked it for eight-thirty.'

'In the morning?!'

'Yes.'

'That's just evil.'

I ended the call with Rosh, and called Ed.

'Ed, it's Adam.'

'Hi.'

'You bastard.'

'Sorry. Sticker collecting is a man's game. I mean, literally speaking it's not, but …'

'I've still got the weekend to find him.'

'Yeah. But you won't.'

'I might.'

'How? What are you going to do – just show up at Oslo airport with a hitchhikers sign saying "Wherever Lars Bohinen's house is"?'

* * * * *

To: FIFA
From: Me
Dear Darth Blatter,
    I'm off to Norway. Travel expenses on the way.
    Cheers,
    Adam
P.S. I've just realised the Cup Winners' Cup was a UEFA competition. Sorry for bothering you about it. My bad.

* * * * *

17 August 2012
Friday (evening)

I had been to Oslo once already, while back packing around Scandinavia a few years previously. It had been cold – too cold to even leave the ho(s)tel, so I had stayed in and watched a Vålerenga game on the television. Everything cost about £10m so I mainly did nothing, as that was one of the few things I could afford to do. After a few days, I packed my bags and left. I vowed not to return unless I had a really good reason to do so. And now I did. Sort of.

I told Anna about my plan. I told her that I was intending to travel to Oslo – the economic and governmental centre of Norway, and the hub of Norwegian trade, banking, industry and shipping, thanks internet! – to try and find Lars Bohinen and take his picture. Anna laughed. Actually laughed, in my face. Not *literally* in my face – she was about four feet away from me – but close enough to my face for it still to count.

She told me she saw a few problems, right off the bat. For one thing, history was against me. Anna reminded me that my previous two ad-hoc visits, to Orpington and Wanfercée-Baulet, had been hugely unsuccessful. When I told her that I wasn't even certain that Lars lived in Oslo, she correctly pointed out that I would probably come back from Norway empty-handed.

We called Lars a few more times. It went to answerphone each and every time. Anna suggested I stay put, and just accept that Ed was probably going to win. I told her I couldn't do that. I told her I was definitely heading to Norway in the morning. Anna let me know that she thought I was doing something stupid and unnecessary. But because she is also an incredibly supportive person, she grabbed a Sharpie and helped me write 'Wherever Lars Bohinen's house is' on a piece of cardboard.

I told Anna I had done some research and, even though I didn't have exact figures, I knew Norway's population was very, very small. Like a thousand people or something. Everyone, therefore, would probably know everyone else and so logically, everyone would probably know where one of the most famous people in the country lived. I would just have to wait until someone offered me a ride.

'Listen,' said Anna. 'I understand you want to beat Ed. But you've already won. You're completing this album the *right way*. You're not just *buying* success, you are *earning* it. You are putting in the hard yards, you're the one making the fruitless and soul-destroying trips over land and sea, you're the one who is *really* experiencing the ups and downs of sticker collecting.

'And you know, deep down, *that* is what is important. You've been on a journey. You have stories to tell. Does it matter if you don't win? Is that really why you started this? Because I'm pretty sure other people completed this album before you.'

I told Anna that there was probably an analogy with football in what she had just said. She told me didn't really care about that, but there was. She asked me if there was anything she could say that would convince me not to go to Norway.

I feigned some chin-stroking deliberation for a while. I sighed deeply a few times, to give the impression that I was seriously considering *not* going to Norway. I started to speak once or twice, only to stop suddenly each time to say something like 'I just don't know' or 'I'm … I just … It's just …' in a stressed sort of way. I told her that in the interest of fairness, I would leave my decision to go to Norway up to a coin toss. Best of five. Heads, I go. Tails, I don't. I fished a coin from my pocket, and flicked it into the air.

Heads.

Flick.

Heads.

Flick.

Heads.

'Shit,' said Anna.

* * * * *

18 August 2012
Saturday

I woke up early – partly because I was nervous, and partly because a low, early morning sunrise was pouring/shining through the slats of my bedroom shutters, and slowly warming my right cheek. Face cheek.

I got up and made some breakfast – blueberry pancakes, crunchy peanut butter on toast, a bowl of muesli and a glass of orange juice. Then I did some other, pretty standard morning activities, like washing myself, getting dressed, and standing in front of the mirror and shouting abuse at the idiot in front of me until he starts to cry.

I include these details for 'characterisation' purposes. Now that you know what I like to eat for breakfast, and the sort of normal everyday routine I have, you know a little more about me. I probably should have done a bit more of that kind of stuff a little earlier, but I never got round to it. Sorry.

I hadn't bought my plane ticket yet. I hadn't even bothered to check the flights. A psychologist/psychiatrist/physiotherapist could probably infer something interesting from my complete lack of forward-planning. Probably awesomeness, or sexiness.

I did, however, have a bit of a plan in mind. The drive from Southsea to Heathrow was around 90 minutes. I planned to arrive, park the car, check the flight times to Oslo, then jump on the first available journey. I got as far as Guildford before I realised flights to Oslo might only go from Gatwick. I decided not to worry about it, and kept going.

I got to Heathrow at around half ten that morning. I parked the car, paid for two days of parking, picked up my 'Wherever Lars Bohinen's house is' sign and my Head travel bag – a relic from my schooldays that still smelt a lot like warm sandwiches and spilt fountain pen ink – and headed into the terminal.

There were flights. There were seats available on those flights. I could afford the price of one of those available seats on one of those flights. There were seats on flights which I could afford which also, luckily, went to Oslo. I was in business, basically. I hope I'm making that clear.

I went to a cash point and withdrew the money I would need for the next two days. Then I went to a bureau de change, and changed it into euros. Then I thought I had better check if Norway used the euro. They didn't. I went back to the bureau de change and changed my euros into Norwegian krone. Then I remembered that in Norway, a chocolate bar costs £250, so I went back to the cash point and got some more money out.

With my bank account now empty and my bum bag now full of unusual money, I sat down in a quiet waiting area and daydreamed for a while. I thought about what I was about to do (meet Lars Bohinen), and where I was about to go (Norway). I thought about everything I had done so far in pursuit of my six stickers (see earlier pages), and how much fun it had been (a lot, even the parts where it went wrong). I thought about the people I had met along the way (all nice, except that juggler guy, Alan, in Belgium, and even he was alright). I felt good. I thought of that James Brown song which perfectly summed up how I was feeling ('Sex Machine').

Then I got a little distracted. I thought about how if you 'tut' without shaking your head at the same time, it looks weird. Then I thought about how strange it is that there are two ways to pronounce the word 'the' – *thee* and *thuh*. And then I thought about how, if there was only *one* pronunciation – *thee* – then so much would be different.

Thuh Beatles would become *Thee* Beatles. Churchill would have told the Nazis we would happily fight them on *thee* beaches. Then I thought that I was allowing my mind to wander a little too far. I reminded myself I had important work to do, and important people to try and see.

I checked the time. It was almost time to go. I checked my phone. There was one text and one e-mail. The text message was long, the e-mail was short. I read both, picked up my things, and set off – happy and excited and utterly certain that I was doing the right thing. This, I thought to myself, was probably how Christopher Columbus felt before he set off looking for the East Indies. Of course, he ended up finding something different altogether. Which is potentially quite a neat little analogy.

* * * * *

The first hour of the journey raced by in a flurry of adrenaline and high-speed travel. The second hour crawled by. Of course, in actual terms, both hours were 60 minutes long. The second hour just *felt* longer. What I'm saying is my perception of each of the two hours was different. Is that relativity? I don't know.

After a little more than two (equally long) hours, I arrived. I collected up my bag and sign, and headed outside into the fresh European air. The sun was shining, the sky was blue: roughly Pantone Sky Blue 14-4318 TPX if you ever feel like recreating the scene on canvas. The gentlest breeze was trying to push a crisp packet around, but the packet was just lying there, not giving a ~~shit~~ hoot. I waited an hour until the crisp packet moved, then focused on the job at hand.

It was 2pm UK time, 3pm Norway time. I texted Anna to let her know I had arrived. She didn't reply. I e-mailed Lars Bohinen, and told him what I was up to, and how he could help. He didn't reply either.

With my bag over my shoulder and my hitchhiker sign in my hand, I walked out towards the main road. It was busy – chocked full of people of all shapes and sizes – but mainly men of average height and ever-so-slightly over-average girth. Waist girth. And as I made my way through them and towards the very edge of the road, I lifted my sign above my head.

Almost immediately, people began to stare. I could tell that a few people recognised the name on the board. I saw a few people grab the arm of their nearest friend, and point them in my direction. I fought an overwhelming urge to stop what I was doing, lower my sign, and throw it into the bin. I reminded myself I had a job to do, and I had travelled a long way in a short time to do it. As a crowd of people streamed past me, I held my ground, and waited.

I wasn't waiting long. A man strolled up to me, with a huge smile in his hand and a briefcase[40] on his face. Something like that anyway. He had seen my sign, and now he had some questions for me. I felt a sickly rush of adrenaline as he approached.

'Excuse me, what is this?' he said, asking his first question. The man was unmistakably English, not Norwegian, which was disappointing. I had met way more Englishmen than Norwegians already, and was hoping to redress the balance.

'Oh, nothing,' I said, quite mentally, considering I was holding a sign asking for directions to Lars Bohinen's home.

'Lars Bohinen,' he said, pointing at the sign. 'Nottingham Forest player, yeah?'

'He was, yeah. Now he is a celebrity ice-skater and commentator. A football commentator, not an ice-skating one, I mean.'

'So what's happening here then? Are you waiting for him?'

'Sort of. It's complicated,' I lied.

The man laughed, and then an uneasy silence fell over the conversation. He stood there, smiling inanely at me, waiting for me to say something. Away in the distance, a police car siren shrieked. As it died away, I told the smiling and staring man all about the Doppler effect. He stopped smiling and staring, and told me he had to leave.

Some minutes passed, as many as pass during an episode of *I'm Alan Partridge*, two-and-a-half episodes of *Marion and Geoff* (series one), or half an episode of *The Wire*.

A few people looked at me funny, but most people just ignored me. I scanned the passing crowd for a helpful face – and when I couldn't find any of those, I scanned for friendly shoulders, arms, knees, fingers, anything. But nobody stopped.

Well, one guy stopped, and was so persistent in his questioning that I told him *exactly* what I was up to. I told him about the sticker

. . . .
40 A briefcase, as promised in the prologue.

album thing and how, after so many months of searching, Lars's was the final picture I needed. He said, 'Stick with it!' I told him that was a pretty awful pun, and as such, I would not be allowing him another line in the book.

Another 15 minutes passed. I checked the time. It was now 2.30pm UK time, 3.30pm Norway time. I kept my sign up with just my right hand – I had been working out a bit, so had the requisite upper body strength to do that – and with my left hand, I got out my phone. I called Lars.

The call didn't connect, so I sent him an e-mail. Then I called Ed. He picked up almost immediately. I asked him if his stickers had arrived yet. He told me he had been out of the house since the early morning, and had missed the morning post. He said he probably wouldn't be returning home until around 9pm UK time, 10pm Norway time, although he might be home as early as 7pm UK time, 8pm Norway time.

He asked me where I was, and I pretended the line was bad and hung up. Or hanged up. I'm not sure which one is right, but the thing to take away from this sentence is that I put the phone down.

I checked the time again. It was nearly 3pm UK time, 4pm Norway time. I had six hours to get Lars's photograph.

So I called him again.

No answer.

And again.

No answer.

And again.

No answer.

And again.

'Hello?'

'Hello, is that Lars?'

'Hi, this is Lars.'

'Hi Lars, it's Adam, the guy writing the book about his old sticker album.'

'Sure. How are you?'

'I'm good. Listen, I've got a favour to ask you …'

And then I asked Lars Bohinen – silky midfielder, ice dancer, protestor against nuclear testing in the South Pacific, the last of my missing six – a huge favour. And he said yes.

I packed up my sign, and placed it neatly in my bag. As I did, a smallish woman, wearing sunglasses and a hat (but nothing else!) approached me.

'Lars Bohinen?' she said, pointing up at the sign with one of her fingers.

'Yeah, Lars Bohinen,' I replied.

'Is that a bum bag you're wearing?' she asked, pointing down at my crotch area with another one of her fingers.

'Yes.'

'I didn't know people still wore those.'

'Some people do, yeah.'

'So: Lars Bohinen is the one who played for Nottingham Forest, right?'

I nodded.

'And Derby County?'

I nodded again.

'And Blackburn Rangers?'

'Rovers,' I said.

'I'm still not certain that's important,' she replied.

And at that moment, I took the smallish woman by the hand, and together, we headed into the stadium.

Because, to be perfectly honest, I wasn't in Oslo.

I wasn't even in Bergen or Trondheim or Grimstad.

I was in England.

I was in Portsmouth.

And I was en route to Fratton Park, to watch my football club play, with my best friend in the world.

Art, 8.

	P	W	D	L	Pts
BROKEN ARM	3	3	0	0	9
SPRAINED ANKLE	3	2	0	1	6
GRAZED KNEE	3	1	0	2	3
STUBBED TOE	3	0	0	3	0

GROUP OF MINOR INJURY.

Twenty-two

I GOT AS far as the airport, but I just couldn't do it. The text message which I received while I was counting out my Norwegian krone was the deal breaker. It was from Anna. She told me that she had bought two tickets for Pompey's opening league game of the season, as a special surprise for me. It was, she said, going to be her first ever live football match. She said she was sorry that they would now go to waste. I felt bad that I had totally forgotten that Pompey were playing that day.

Obviously, there was only one thing I could do. I couldn't let Anna down. I got back in my car, turned my sat-nav on and, for once, listened to Homer as he told me to turn around. But honestly, I wasn't just turning around because I didn't want to disappoint Anna.

I was turning around because Portsmouth, not Oslo, was where I should have been. I hadn't been here enough while the shit was hitting the fan. I had forgotten that it was here, inside the ground, at a live football match, that the real magic happened.

I texted Anna and told her I would meet her near Frogmore Road. I told her to look for an idiot holding a sign with the words 'Wherever Lars Bohinen's house is' written on it. She found me with ease. There were no more than two or three people holding the same sign.

Anna and I took our seats at the back of the South Stand, and watched the game. Pompey had somehow cobbled together a side made up of free transfers and loans and pre-pubescent youth team players. Even the mascot had a squad number. But Fratton Park was packed, every corner chocked full of passionate and pissed off fans, happy to see their side still in existence, but acutely aware of just how dire the situation still was. I realised

238

just how much I would have missed all this, if the club had gone to the wall.

The noise was deafening and the sunshine glorious, from minute one to minute 94. In minute 19, Pompey went ahead, when a shot from Izale McLeod squirmed through the hands of Bournemouth keeper Shwan Jalal and into the net. Up until minute 45, Pompey were superb. From minutes 46 to 77, Bournemouth came back into it. And in minute 78, Lee Barnard, a Southampton loanee, equalised for the Cherries. By minute 94, Anna was delirious. I asked her to sum up the experience in one word.

'Amazing,' she said.

'OK, now sum up the experience in two words,' I said.

'Really amazing.'

'Five words.'

'Really, really, really, really, amazing.'

'Ten words.'

'*Really* amazing. Stop asking me to describe it …'

I told her that was only eight words.

'… you dick,' she added.

As we made our way back to our flat, Anna asked me if I thought I had made the right decision not to go to Norway. I told her I thought I had. She pointed out that I was now almost certainly going to lose to Ed. I told her to stop taking the gloss off a really brilliant afternoon.

And then, for the rest of the walk home, I listened as she excitedly talked me through her highlights of the game. I smiled, from ear to ear (figuratively), as Anna told me that the last few hours, spent in a rickety old stadium, sat on agonising blue plastic seats, watching a football match between two teams in the third tier of the English football pyramid, was the most fun she'd had in ages. She wanted to come back, as soon as possible. She told me she finally understood why I was so smitten with the game, and why I was so worried that feeling might have been on the wane. And even though she knew the standard was probably higher elsewhere, at Manchester United and Chelsea and what-have-you, she said she didn't care.

She realised that Pompey would probably lose more often than they would win, but she just enjoyed being at the stadium.

She just enjoyed watching football. She enjoyed the camaraderie and the singing and the sense of community. She said she felt like she was part of a club, of something bigger than the sum of its parts. I told her I did too.

As we sat down in the lounge of the flat, Anna checked through the morning's post. There was another letter for me. By now, the handwriting was familiar, as were the contents. So much so, that I didn't even bother to open it. I knew Peter Atherton's head was inside. I knew I still didn't need it. I still had no idea why I kept getting it through the post.

I felt my phone vibrate in my pocket. I checked the time on the clock on the wall opposite. It was 7pm. It was probably Ed, calling to tell me he had arrived home, found the package with his two stickers inside and stuck them into his now-completed album. I reluctantly pulled the phone out of my jeans.

But it wasn't Ed, calling.

It was Lars Bohinen, e-mailing.

He was doing me the small favour I had asked of him earlier in the day.

It was a simple sort of e-mail.

But then, that's all I had asked him for.

I had told him that I wasn't going to make it to Norway after all.

But while I wasn't coming to visit him, I still needed a photo.

I needed him to take a little snap of himself.

And e-mail it to me.

I told him I was up against a deadline.

I *might* (did) tell him it was a print deadline for this book.

It wasn't.

It was a deadline to beat Ed in the race to complete our sticker album first.

I opened the e-mail.

And this is what it looked like.

From: Lars Bohinen
To: Me
Maybe you can use this?

When I saw it, I did four things. First, I let out a loud cheer. Second, I replied to Lars, and thanked him profusely for taking a picture of himself and sending it through so promptly. Thirdly, I gave Anna a huge, celebratory kiss and told her, at long last, that I was in love with her. And fourthly, I called Ed. He picked up after one ring.

'Ed, it's Adam. Listen, I can't chat for long as I'm very busy, but I just thought I should let you know that I've spoken to Lars Bohinen. I asked him to take a picture of himself, then e-mail it through to me so I could make the last sticker for my album.'

'Hi mate, I can't hear you. Call me back in five minutes.'

I put the phone down.

Five minutes passed.

I called Ed again.

He picked up after one ring.

'Ed, it's Adam. Listen, I can't chat for long as I'm very busy, but I just thought I should let you know that I've spoken to Lars Bohinen. I asked him to take a picture of himself, then e-mail it through to me so I could make the last sticker for my album.'

'And? Has he done it?'

'Yes. Yes, he has.'

Ed said nothing. I asked him what expression was on his face, right now. He said it was 'disappointment at [his] impending defeat in the race to complete *Premier League 96*'. I told him that was quite a specific facial expression. He admitted it was a first for him.

'So you've done it?' he said. 'You've completed the album?'

'No, not quite yet,' I said. 'I still have to print it out and stick it in.'

'So do it.'

'I can't. We don't have a printer here. The only one is at my parents' house.'

'And how far away is your parents' house?'

'Twenty minutes, by car.'

'Interesting,' said Ed. I heard the sound of an engine revving in the background. 'Because I'm *ten* minutes away from *my* house.'

'Oh.'

'Yeah. And I don't have to print out anything. I just have to open my mail, and stick the stickers in.'

'Assuming they've arrived.'

'Exactly.'

'So, what, this is some sort of climactic car chase now, is it?' I asked.

'Looks like it. A climactic car chase to reach a printer, and a piece of unopened post.'

'Classic.'

'Yeah.'

'OK, drive safely,' I said.

'You too,' said Ed.

I jumped in the car, put on Otis Redding's 'Can't Turn You Loose', then drove like the wind (i.e. fast, but safe) back to my parents' house.

Along the way, I accidentally ran a red light and was chased by a string of police cars. Keen to get to my parents' house before Ed, miles away in north London, got back to his flat, I led the cops on a madcap chase through a shopping mall, during which time I caused damage worth hundreds of thousands of pounds to (in actual order) Toys R' Us, a flower stall, a formalwear store, a bakery, a music store, a bridal shop, some sort of picture frame seller, a car dealership, a little hut selling t-shirts and finally a newsagent, before smashing my way through the window of a department store and onwards to my goal.

As I raced through Portsmouth and onwards to my childhood home – the place, you'll no doubt remember, where I found the album in the first place – the traffic slowed to a snail's pace (approximately 0.03mph), then sped up slightly to a giant galapagos tortoise's pace (about 1mph) then dropped right down to a coral's pace (coral doesn't move, duh). For five minutes, we didn't move either. The climactic car chase was going quite slowly.

I called Ed. Well, Anna did. I was in control of a motor vehicle and did not have a hands-free kit. After a few seconds, Anna told me he wasn't answering, which was either the truth, or a kind lie to shield me from the fact Ed had answered his phone and screamed 'I AM THE WINNER!' down the phone. I asked Anna what we should do. She said we should wait. The traffic would move soon enough. We were a little more than a mile away from home and possible glory.

Another two minutes passed. Anna called Ed again. I guessed that he probably answered this time, because quite suddenly, Anna told me to take the next left into a nondescript residential road, park up, and get ready to run. So I did. And we did.

We sprinted past the queues of cars, and the roadworks responsible. We squinted into the slow-setting sun as we pounded the pavement towards home. We skirted round mums with pushchairs and weaved between kids on bikes, until my parents' road was within sight.

We rounded the bend and hot-footed it into the back corner of the cul-de-sac, and with my keys already drawn, bounded up the stone steps (posh, right?) and into my parents' house. I leapt up the stairs, two at a time, and Anna followed behind. I was too busy rushing about to count how many steps she took at a time. Sorry.

I skidded into the spare room, and fairly punched the computer on. Then I kicked the printer into life, and, in a fit of impatience, shouted needlessly negative things at the mouse. All three sprang into life quickly enough, and I surfed my way to my e-mails, found the one from Lars, clicked on his photo, waited a split-second for it to download, then opened it, re-sized it, and thumped ctrl and P.

The printer whirred into life. A few seconds later, a perfect, sticker-sized photo of Lars Bohinen dropped into the print tray. I snatched it up, and in the absence of some scissors, tried to free-hand tear it out. Anna took the paper, folded around Lars's picture like some sort of origami ninja, and quickly (and quite violently) tore it free.

I emptied out the drawers of the computer table, but found no sticky tape or glue or anything. So I flipped out another couple of drawers, much to the chagrin – no, absolute disgust is truer – of my parents downstairs, who were now quite alarmed by all the commotion I was making. Again, I could find no material with which I could stick one bit of paper to another.

Anna rifled through her bag. She found a packet of chewing gum. She popped a bit in her mouth, chewed it for a second, then threw it over to me. Normally she is classier than that, but she's also the most awesome person in the world, and as the most awesome person in the world, she appreciated that this situation required her to act like this.

I caught the gum, stuck it to the back of Lars's head, flipped open *Premier League 96* – I had been carrying that the whole time, obviously – to the Blackburn pages, found Lars's gap, lined him up and stuck him home.

My phone vibrated. It was Ed. I picked it up, and before he could speak, opened my lungs and loudly celebrated/gloated about my victory. From the other end of the phone, I heard a roughly approximate noise. It was guttural and growly and definitely a little gloaty.

'What did you just say?' I asked, at the same time Ed asked me the exact same question.

'I didn't so much *say* anything as just sort of cheer,' replied Ed.

'Me too.'

'Oh. So does that mean …?'

'Yeah. I've finished the album. I just stuck the last sticker in. With chewing gum, actually.'

'Well, I've finished too.'

'Oh.'

'Yeah.'

'So …?' I said, hoping Ed would be a gentleman and simply admit that I had *actually* won.

'Call it a draw, then?' he said, very much *not* admitting that I had actually won.

'I suppose so,' I replied.

'This is a bit of an anti-climax, isn't it?'

'A bit.'

We both fell silent for a bit.

'Best of three?' said Ed.

* * * * *

19 August 2012
Sunday

'A great plan? No,' said Rosh.

'Yes it was,' I replied. 'It was *great*. Like Operation Mincemeat, or the Trojan Horse.'

'Both great plans. But this …'

'This was as good, and much simpler. No subterfuge. No slaughter. No woodworking. Actually, there was some mild subterfuge. And I killed a moth in Belgium. But no woodworking.'

'I still don't understand why you had to do all of this.'

'Because it was incomplete, Rosh. I needed to complete the album because it was incomplete.'

'But wasn't there more to it than that?'

'Not really.'

'Haven't you learned that football has been utterly destroyed by greed and excess?'

'Nope.'

'Have you realised that you *really* wanted to spend all this time completing your album because you were anxious about becoming a proper adult?'

'Nah.'

'Alright, well have you learned that nostalgia is a dangerous and often misleading thing?'

'Only a bit.'

'Have you grown as a person in some way along the course of this little adventure?'

'Not particularly.'

Rosh exhaled loudly, 'Have you learned *anything*?'

'I think so. I think I've finally realised, for the first time ever, what it is I love about football. And I've also realised that the things that I love about the game, are the same things that have been missing from my personal life too.'

'Really?!'

'Nah. It was just about the stickers. Anyway, I have to go now. I'm about to throw my sticker album into the Solent.'

'What?'

'I have to go and throw my sticker album into the Solent. It's a sort of symbolic thing to do.'

'A *symbolic thing to do*? Is that a joke!?'

'No, it's a symbolic action. Now, the Scottish Premier League, *that* is a jo…'

Right then, and without hesitation, Rosh ended the call. I was secretly quite relieved. I felt as though I had made that Scottish Premier League joke enough already.

I slipped my phone back into my pocket, and turned to Anna, who had been patiently sat beside me while I called Rosh and told him my sticker collecting quest was finally over. A gentle breeze whipped across the beach.

'Ready?' she asked.

'Ready,' I said.

In front of me, stretching out towards the horizon like a massive and wet and poorly signposted road, was the Solent. I held *Premier League 96* like a discus in my right hand and took a few practice swings.

Yes, it *did* feel like quite a weird thing to be doing, but somehow it was also strangely in keeping with the whole adventure so far. It was a strange and quite possibly unnecessary exercise, but I was happy to go with it. It was something new. I had definitely never thrown a football album into a large body of water before.

I took a few steps back from the edge of the water. Pebbles crunched and clacked beneath my feet. There was no sound, apart from the soothing sigh of the sea lapping at the shore, and the faraway *nee-naw-nee-naw-nee-naw* of a fire engine. I took a deep breath, closed my eyes, and pulled my arm back. The album was finally complete. It was time to throw it away. It was time to move on.

But before I could swing through and send the album to its watery end, a voice shouted out to stop.

It was Anna.

She said she had a confession to make.

She reached into her bag, and pulled out an envelope.

Inside the envelope was a sticker.

A sticker I had seen before.

Often enough that, by this point, it was starting to get a little weird.

It was Peter Atherton.

'Why is *he* here again?!' I asked.

'I *really* hoped it wouldn't come to this. I tried to make it obvious. I made it *so* obvious!' she said.

'What are you talking about?'

'Who do you think was sending you the Peter Atherton stickers?!'

'Jay in Belgium?'

'Nope.'

'No?'

'Nope.'

'Alan Risley-Tan?'

'Nope.'

'No?'

'Nope. It was me.'

'You?!'

'Yes. I bought it. I was the one who kept trying to give it to you.'

'But why?!'

'Turn to the Sheffield Wednesday page,' said Anna.

I turned to the Sheffield Wednesday page.

'Now look for the Peter Atherton sticker.'

I looked for the Peter Atherton sticker.

'Is it there?' she asked.

'No. John Sheridan is where Peter Atherton should be. I've stuck two John Sheridans on the same page …'

'Yeah. You have.'

'Fuck.'

'I guess 12-year-old Adam must have got a little confused. I noticed it months ago. I was trying to draw your attention to it. But you *never* quite got the message.'

'You could have just told me!' I said.

'Nah. This way was more fun.'

I nodded. Anna was absolutely right. This way *was* more fun. She moved closer, whispered in my ear that 'Alan Risley-Tan' was actually an anagram of 'It's Really Anna' and placed the Peter Atherton sticker in my hand. She told me to stick him home so my album could finally be officially full.

I didn't. Instead, I swung my sticker album behind my head, and threw it into the sea. Anna laughed. That happy and familiar feeling in the pit of my stomach – the same one I had felt on my first visit to Fratton Park and when I had first met Anna – came rushing back. I told Anna that I was ridiculously in love with her, and then we went home to our flat, stuck Athers on the fridge for safe-keeping and ate some pizza. It was a pretty good day.

* * * * *

To: FIFA

From: Me

Dear Mr Blatter,

My album is complete. Shouldn't I be winning some sort of FIFA Outstanding Achievement award for this?

Yours in expectation of an award for this,

Adam

Art, 9.

THE POZNAN.
(REVERSE VIEW)

Epilogue

So, THE album was complete at last. Or at least, every space was filled. Peter Atherton was missing, but that didn't matter. My aim was to meet the six players missing from the album when I found it, and I had achieved that. Well, I didn't *actually* achieve that, but I *did* get a photograph of each of them – even if I wasn't there to take Lars's photo personally. The whole thing was certainly closer to a success than it was a failure. Which really should be Pompey's (and my own) motto. I might suggest it at a supporters' meeting soon.

A lot has happened since my album disappeared into the sea. Pompey are still a football club. They were relegated to League 2 at the end of the 2012/13 season, which meant that, for the first time since before I was born, the club would be playing fourth division football.

But truthfully, the news from Fratton Park has been almost universally positive in the months since the end of this little story. The fan buy-out went through in April 2013, making Pompey the largest fan-owned football club in British football. Which is nice. Yes, we'll probably be shit for a good few years. But honestly, does that matter? Of course not.

Pompey are now owned and run by the fans, for the fans. It feels like the start of a brave and bold new era. I chipped in and part-own a share of the club. I plan to use my not inconsiderable power for good. I also plan to go to Fratton Park more.

It took Anna's wide-eyed wonder to make me realise it, but that's where the real magic happens. Not in the pub, not on the TV, but in the stadium, in the thick of the din, among the petrifying Pompey kids who know the referee is a wanker long before they know where South America is (near North America), or how many wives Henry VIII had (six).

Speaking of which, Ed and I are still great mates. We have agreed that our sticker collecting days are now behind us. We still argue over who 'won' the sticker race. I told him about the Peter Atherton thing in the end. As a result, he claims I didn't 'officially' complete the album, while I argue that he is an idiot for saying that.

We're arguing about it less and less, though. Now we both tend to agree that we are both losers for caring so much in the first place. We also, quite secretly, believe that our collecting days might *not* be fully behind us yet. That 'best of three' suggestion is still under consideration.

I haven't stayed in touch with any of the footballers, but each and every one of them was so friendly and accommodating and bright and just plain nice that if you ever bump into any of them, buy them a beer. They deserve it. They had to put up with my e-mails and phone calls and tweets. And if you see Peter Atherton – or if you know him personally – tell him to contact me. I would love to buy him a beer, too. Unfortunately, Mr Blatter has not replied to any of my e-mails yet.

Jay from Belgium is getting married. He has invited me to the wedding. He is not a robot. I checked, as I promised I would. I was very thorough. Too thorough, maybe. Alan, Jay's juggler mate, is 'performing' at the reception. I intend to go and throw things at him. If he's a proper juggler, he'll incorporate them into his routine. If he isn't, they will just smack him in the face. I still hate jugglers. I'm still not entirely sure why.

I don't work for Rosh anymore. My contract came to an end, and I fancied a change. So did Rosh. He and I are still good friends though. By which I mean I think he's great, and he thinks I'm a flipping idiot. We're both wrong, I think. He has read this book, and has told me I should have developed the whole 'me working for him' into a more developed story arc. I have admitted that I didn't, because I couldn't be bothered.

And in case you're curious, I *still* don't know the nature of the 'personal reasons' that prevent my mum from washing my pants.

But most importantly of all, Anna and I are still very much together. In fact, since the end of this book, things have progressed very quickly for us as a couple. We officially moved in together in January 2013. Around about that time, I had a few conversations with myself about proposing to her sometime very soon. I allowed myself to daydream about starting a family with her one day too.

In February 2013, Anna fell pregnant. With a baby. Human. A human baby. A human baby girl. I am the impregnator. Anna prefers 'father'. I proposed not long after – not because of the pregnancy, this isn't Puritan England in the 17th century, granddad – but because, as this book hopefully demonstrates in some small way, she is the kindest, most supportive and fun and clever and interesting and sweet and hilarious person on the planet. She said yes, by the way.

Since the day I met her, I've not doubted for an instant that she is the one for me. The first draft of this book (ha, the very idea I wrote more than one draft is laughable, but go with it) was over 400,000 words long, and most of that was taken up with epic poems dedicated to Anna and how ruddy excellent she is. She is my best friend, my biggest supporter, my closest confidante, my fairest critic, a constant source of inspiration and pride and generally everything any decent human would aspire to be. And she's easy on the eye, too. I'm a fan, basically.

We are now married. We have bought a flat in Southsea, near the sea. Not so near that we have to worry about coastal erosion or tidal waves or sharknadoes, but near enough. It is nice. I am sitting in it right now (I mean 'right now' while I type this, not necessarily 'right now' while you're reading).

So, why did I collect the stickers? Thankfully, I've finally worked it out. It's horribly simple, I'm afraid.

The answer is:

Because it was a fun thing to do.

There really wasn't a deeper meaning than that. But does there have to be?

The supposedly 'deeper meanings' I tried to attribute to this quest have all fallen by the wayside. In the end, this wasn't about a desire to reconnect with the football of my youth. It wasn't about trying to track the myriad changes that have taken place in the game in the past few decades. It wasn't even about trying to find the lost 'soul' of football. It was just about having some fun, and going on a bit of an adventure.

But that, in itself, has been a discovery. I have realised that football doesn't always need deeper meanings. It doesn't need great and grand narratives to be interesting. Sometimes, it's alright for it just to be a game – albeit a bloody good one.

I have realised that football *should* be fun, that supporting your club *should* be a bit of an adventure, just like all this sticker album nonsense was. I have realised that football *doesn't* annoy me, I was just focusing on the external noise that surrounds the modern game. I have realised I was never out of love with football, I just forgot *what* I loved about it in the first place.

So dig out your own ancient albums. See how many stickers you still need. Then go on an adventure. Or better yet, get to your nearest stadium, buy a ticket and just watch, and enjoy. After all, that's the point. Being a football fan is an opportunity – a chance to laugh and cry and whinge and explore and connect with new people. Take it.

As I write this, our little daughter's due date is still two months away. When I started out on this little sticker book quest, I was obsessed with the idea of meeting six strangers. I ended up meeting my soulmate, and making a brand new human with her. I am pretty pleased with that.

But if the little 'un ever decides she wants to collect stickers, I will warn her that they can be quite addictive. And then I will make sure that whatever collection she has is absolutely bloody complete before it gets packed away in a box in the attic.

Or maybe I won't.

Maybe I'll make sure she leaves a few gaps.

A final realisation

'Adam?'

'Yes, Anna?'

'You know when you were in Manchester, and Stuart Ripley called you just as you were about to give up and head back home?'

'Yes.'

'Well, I've been thinking – Stuart did not have your mobile number. He couldn't have. You didn't send it to him on your initial e-mail.'

'Didn't I?'

'No, I've just checked.'

'Oh.'

'So it can't have been him calling you.'

'But I saved that number in my phone as "Stuart Ripley".'

'Have you ever called it?'

'No.'

'Shall we call it now? Just to check. It won't be him though.'

'OK.'

I called the number and waited.

It wasn't Stuart.

It was Peter Atherton.

No, not really. It was my friend Robyn. She had been calling to tell me that she had just changed numbers. I told her that without that call, I might never have completed my *Premier League 96* sticker album. I began to tell her the story you've just read. She told me she had another call coming in, and had to go. She hasn't called since.

Thank you

Huge thanks to Anna, Pip, Mum, Dad, Josh, Grandma, all of the McBrides and Sharples, all of the wonderful press officers at the various clubs who helped, Richard Martin, Richard Edwards, Ed and Georgie, Jason and Holly, Rosh, the tremendously talented Stassja Mrozinski who designed the stickers and helped design the front cover, Mr and Mrs Engo and the two smaller Engos, all six of the footballers who were so tremendously helpful and friendly, and all at Pitch for the support and patience.

ADAM CARROLL-SMITH is an author and sports journalist who lives in Southsea. *Six Stickers* is Adam's second book, following the acclaimed *Chasing Sachin*, which saw him trailing his boyhood hero Sachin Tendulkar around the country. At school, Adam was voted 'Most Likely to Write About Himself in the Third Person on a Book Jacket'. You can find him on Twitter: @ACarrollSmith.